DAYS TO REMEMBER

America 1945-1955

by

John Gunther & Bernard Quint

Harper & Brothers   *Publishers*   New York

Library of Congress catalog card number: 56-8751

Acknowledgments

The authors join the publisher in acknowledging a special indebtedness to "Life" for permission to use a major selection of pictures which are the property of the magazine—and more especially to the "Life" photographers without whose skillful world coverage no book such as this would be possible. The authors alone bear responsibility for the editorial content and design of this book. Our "credit" page will also reveal our debt to the major picture agencies and free-lance photographers.

We are indebted to Doris O'Neil, whose excellence in picture research has made an invaluable contribution to this book, and to Beverly Baff Quint and Jane Gunther for their patience and advice.

"The Information Please Almanac," "The World Almanac" and "Facts on File" have been indispensable in checking facts and chronology. Also we want to thank Miss Marguerite Hoyle of Harper & Brothers for her help in research.

The Authors

Foreword

The purpose of this book is to reflect and recall ten of the most crowded and fascinating years in our history—to depict in pictures and text what seized public attention in politics, entertainment, fads and fancies, foreign policy, race relations, and much else in the glowing panorama of American life. In a sense, this post-World War II decade was a veritable "American Decade" all over the free world.

World War II ended on the deck of an American ship after a victory made possible largely by American industrial, scientific and military might (although the atomic bomb was in fact a truly international invention). Then, for a time, we tried to withdraw from the world scene. Americans coveted nobody else's land or wealth. We occupied enemy lands with distinct uneasiness, and we sat on international tribunals as awkward and untried participants. But before the decade was half done, the U.S. was manifestly the great power in all of the non-Communist world. Our influence ranged from Tokyo to Berlin, from Arctic Norway to the Australasian Antipodes. We dominated the free world almost in spite of ourselves. And at home, we were growing and changing with incredible velocity.

This was the decade of the Salk vaccine and of the Supreme Court ban on segregation, of brilliantly exciting baseball and pre-frozen food, of automation, glass skyscrapers and backyard swimming pools, of bulging colleges, television, wide-screen movies, and the peaceful application of nuclear energy. It was also, in part at least, a decade of fear. Not since post-Civil War days have we known such distrust among neighbors. Blame it on what you will—first of course on our continuing discovery of the nature of Communism; or on the treasonable actions or carelessness of men who had seemed beyond reproach, or the urge of others to capitalize on their own "Americanism" through reckless smear charges. But soon we seemed to be regaining our confidence and sense of balance. Also, while given to a surface uniformity, we showed again and again that we were actually a people of the most infinite variety. Even our admiration for material progress was demonstrably accompanied by a deep spiritual hunger which revealed itself in various forms. In little ways and big, we hurried eagerly down fresh paths, even if we weren't always sure, and sometimes didn't care, where they led.

This book is an attempt to see whether by visual emphasis we can render the decade more vivid than we could by emphasis on words alone; also, while the decade is still very close to our minds, to present it so that it may become more meaningful in a positive sense. There have been times in the past ten years when almost every adult American was "sweating it out" in one sense or another, but we have met successfully a lot of lively and bewildering challenges, and we've often had fun doing it. We've made mistakes, yes, but so does everybody. If we see how well we did manage to deal with the challenges of the last ten years, perhaps we'll have a better perspective on the challenges of the next and next.

The Authors

Florida

The War is Over!

The War is Over!

And so World War II died. "Died" is not an altogether inappropriate word, since, to most Americans, the war had become a kind of monstrous living thing—an octopus, a ferocious beast eating time, our dreams, money, ambition, leisure, lives. But also the war gave unity to the nation, stimulated it to vast prodigies of endeavor, lit it up with an incandescent patriotism, and gave it point, pith, direction, and an immeasurable emotional upthrust. Some people even liked it. Perhaps that is the worst thing about war—that some people can't help liking it. But let us remember that World War II cost us more than 400,000 lives.

In any case we had to win it, and we did. The monster had to be killed, and we killed it. And volcanic enthusiasm greeted the event. The country felt the kind of relief that comes to a feverish sick person when the fever, at long last, breaks. We became bathed in the sudden miraculous sweat of convalescence. Americans are a people notorious for their love of happy endings, and we kissed our wives or anybody else, got drunk, jumped naked into pools, and tossed fireplugs through the windows of the nearest Five and Ten.

Yet there were few organized parades, and, once the V-J spurt of excitement passed, comparatively little broad-scale jubilance. Perhaps we were too numbed by all that we had been through. The mood of the country was sober rather than exuberant. What were we going to do with the priceless boon of peace? Would we be able to measure up to our responsibilities as the greatest power on earth? Were we seasoned enough, mature enough,

Pearl Harbor

New York

San Francisco

7

to hold this new position unparalleled in our or anybody's history? We had the machines and men, but did we have the brains, the imagination, the good will?

All this—the victorious end of the greatest war in history—occurred a little more than a decade ago. It is a strange experience to look back and rediscover days that, to some of us, already seem to be almost

inconceivably remote.

S.S. guards set fire to prisoners' barracks, to prevent liberation by advancing U.S. troops.

Mussolini and his mistress hang upside down. So a disgraceful death comes to enemy dictator.

The pace of events has never been sharper, faster, more cutting than in this turbulent mid-century decade. In **1945** Eisenhower still wore a uniform, and Stevenson and Kefauver were virtually unknown on the national scene. The phrases "Cold War" and "Iron Curtain" were still unborn. Nobody had ever heard of Grace Kelly, canasta, or streptomycin, and we did not know much about guided missiles. Korea was a little-known peninsula somewhere in Asia, and few would have recognized the names of Whittaker Chambers or Alger Hiss. We did not know in 1945 that the United States would soon be spending forty billions a year on national defense, and that the American frontier would stretch from Okinawa to outposts near the Rhine.

We knew in 1945 some of the things behind us. Gross villains like Mussolini and Hitler had been dispatched at last, and the mass extermination of the innocent by dogma-crazed dictators would occur no more. But we did not know what was before us.

Never have years been so crowded and fruitful with challenge. The first decade of peace, the first ten years of the atomic age, beckoned to us with a fierce, drastic urgency.

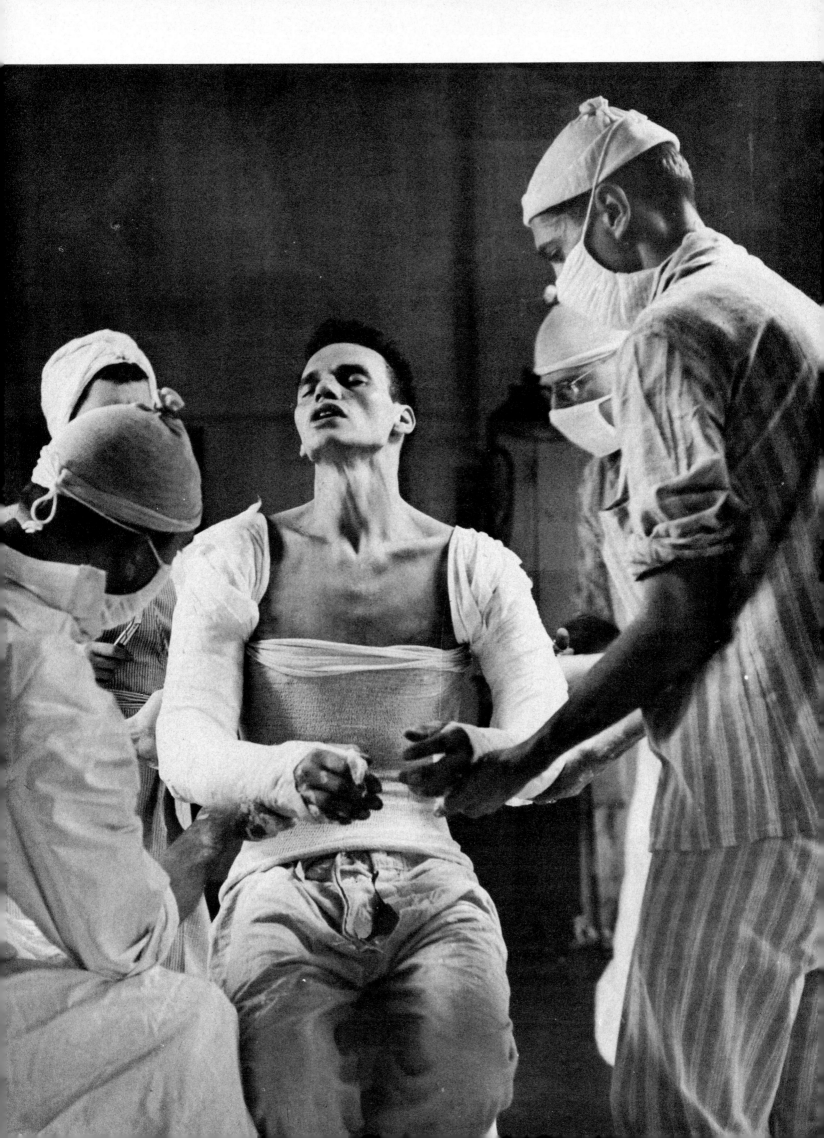

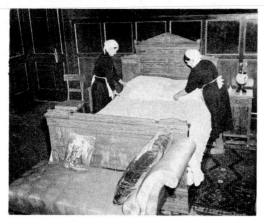

Roosevelt's bed at Yalta.

FDR, Eleanor, and Fala take a moment off from burdens at Hyde Park.

We begin, now, with the later months of **1945**. The American people plunged into the more immediate problems of reconversion, to unshackle the giant machine that had brought victory. Reconversion took place on almost every level—from the dismantling of robot-like munitions plants to the painful, laborious rebuilding of individual human minds and bodies. This was a war which had taken a real bite out of the United States.

Specifically, what were some of the new challenges? First, to make peace stick. And even before Yalta it had become ominously apparent that Russia, the wartime ally, was not going to be a gracious bedfellow. Second, to maintain ample strength, in case peace did not stick. But GI's by the million were clamoring to come home, the Navy went into mothballs, and citizens yelled for nylons, automobiles, and iceboxes. Third, to keep the economy advancing, to keep the standard of living high, to make the limitless riches of America available to the maximum number of people. But what about taxes, prices, and inflation? Fourth, to preserve fully and uncompromisingly our democratic liberties, which had survived the war, in what came to be circumstances of unparalleled assault and strain. There were ^{ugly} *shadows in the wings.*

Fifth, to see to it that man remained master of his new machines, and not vice versa.

1945 held events great and small. Roosevelt died, and the San Francisco Conference established the UN. Lend-Lease ended, and the trials of Nazi, Fascist, and Japanese war criminals began. Never before had civilian leaders of a defeated country been brought before courts of justice administered by the victors. Louis Budenz, editor of the "Daily Worker," broke with the Communist party, thus setting a fashion in political apostasy. Barbara Hutton divorced Cary Grant, her third husband, because "he made her rather nervous." Dow-Jones averages stood at 169.89, and novels were still selling for $2.50. Cordell Hull won the Nobel peace prize, and Douglas MacArthur started a land reform system in Japan. And, incredible as the fact may seem, the country had six commercial TV stations—imagine! To the wonders of the new world there seemed no end.

The nation weeps as Roosevelt, only man ever to be President of U.S. four times, goes to his grave.

Surgeons strap wounded G.I. into cast. This was a war that hurt almost everybody.

Truman was still Vice-President when a lady soon to become Mrs. Humphrey Bogart gave accolade to his piano playing.

Harry Truman's boyhood teachers learn that he is President, and do not seem particularly surprised.

Roosevelt's death had occurred early in the year, a few weeks before V-E Day and a few months before V-J Day. It is difficult, if not impossible, to assess his contribution in a paragraph. He was a patrician who became a man of the people. He did not have the use of his legs, but this did not keep him from making more of an impact on America than any President since Lincoln. He took office during the most grievous economic depression the nation had ever known, and managed to keep it afloat without any compromise of civil liberties. He led the nation into war, and was a prime architect of victory. Urbane, buoyant, courageous, he had surpassing charm and some pettinesses, and was one of the most masterful practical politicians ever to function in this republic.

Mrs. Roosevelt's first words after her husband's death were, "I am more sorry for the people of the country than I am for us." When Mr. Truman hurried over to the White House he asked her,

"What can I do?"

Her reply was, "Tell us what we can do. Is there any way we can help you?"

Roosevelt was gone, and whether you liked him or not he left a vacuum. What would we do without him? What was Truman going to be like?

America's Ike, home in triumph, is greeted by New York's Little Flower. One of Eisenhower's first statements: "No intelligent person can be isolationist."

Atom bomb explodes over Bikini—

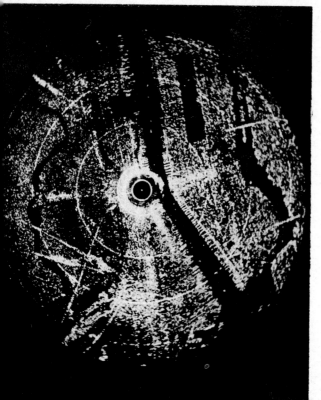

New York City looks this way, photographed by radar.

The first atomic bomb fused the earth at Alamogordo, New Mexico, on July 16, 1945, and the world will never be the same again. This man-made

fragment of the sun ended the war

against Japan. Today bombs are inconceivably more powerful as well as easier to deliver. So it may be pertinent to recall that the puny, minuscule bomb exploded over Hiroshima on August 6, 1945, killed 78,150 people in the flash of a second; the one dropped on Nagasaki a few days later killed 73,844.

At once the bomb changed all patterns not merely in national defense but in world politics. Possession of the bomb by the United States and our allies was, during the first Cold War period, the decisive deterrent to Soviet aggression. When, a few years later, our monopoly ended, an entirely new and frightening phase in international relations perforce began.

The bomb not only opened avenues to new and hideous ways of warfare;

—sunrise or sunset for mankind?

it gave promise, if only mankind had sense enough, to transform utterly the world of peace, by opening unparalleled new opportunities in the creation of wealth and leisure. And it may bring to light some of the blackest secrets of disease, and save millions of lives thereby. Moreover the bomb (using the word "bomb" to symbolize nuclear energy) became not only the most formidable engine of destruction the world has ever known, but potentially the greatest agent for peace. For the first time in the history of the world, each side in a major war now has the means not merely for vanquishing but for obliterating the other and destroying civilization to boot. A little anecdote is told about Professor Einstein. Somebody asked him what the weapons of World War III would be. He replied, "I do not know. But I do know what the weapons of World War IV will be. Rocks."

Meantime wraps were taken off arcane inventions like radar. But Americans adjust to miracles rapidly. Announcement came that radar contact with the moon had been established, and hardly anybody batted an eye.

Navy doctors test hapless goat for radiation effects.

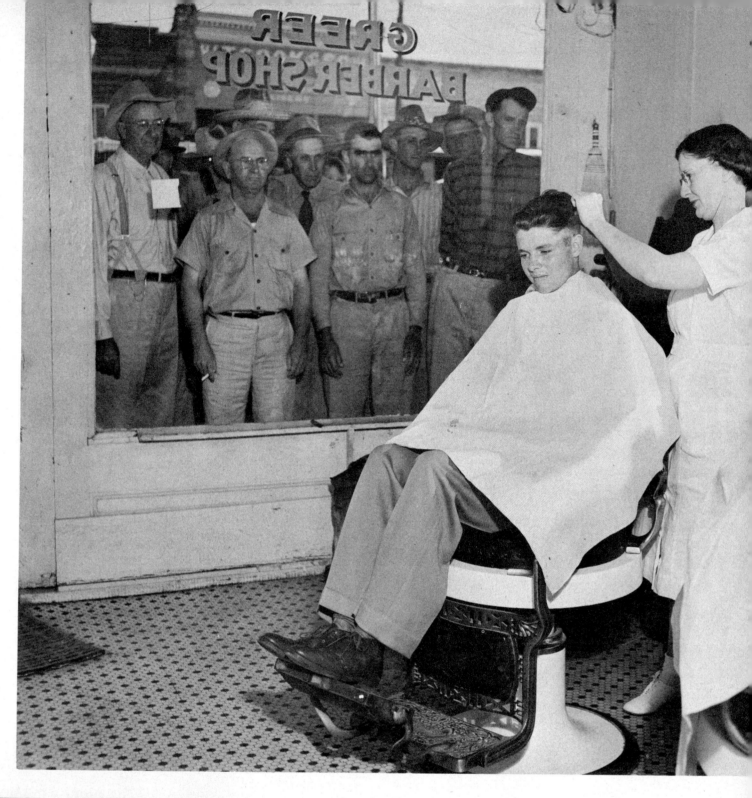

Iowa students hire stenographers to take down lecture notes, then sell them to next year's class. G.I.'s all over the country were crazy to catch up with education.

On the home front, as **1945** merged into **1946**, millions of GI's sought readjustment and reincorporation into the life of their communities. Maybe that old job was *waiting for them,* and maybe not. Maybe that old girl was waiting for them, or maybe they had forgotten that old girl. Some veterans cracked up, filled the hospitals, and foreshadowed grave problems in public health. Some got married, lifted the birthrate to unprecedented levels, complained at prices, and otherwise had fun, if they were not too disoriented. A prevailing keynote was thirst for education. The GI Bill of Rights opened university doors on a scale never known

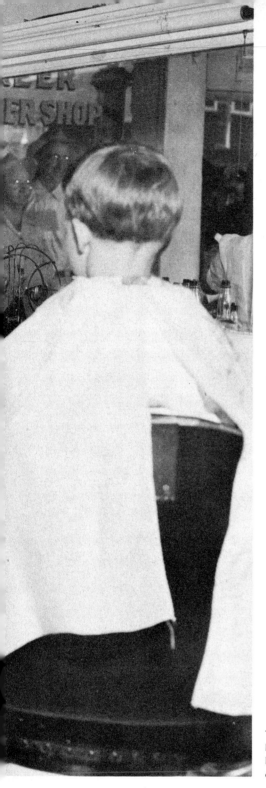

Shirley Temple, 17, married Air Force
Sergeant John Agar, 24.
Thousands of Hollywood fans sought
to storm the church.
Shirley, who earned $3,000,000 before
she was eleven, was "cool and poised."

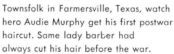

Townsfolk in Farmersville, Texas, watch
hero Audie Murphy get his first postwar
haircut. Same lady barber had
always cut his hair before the war.

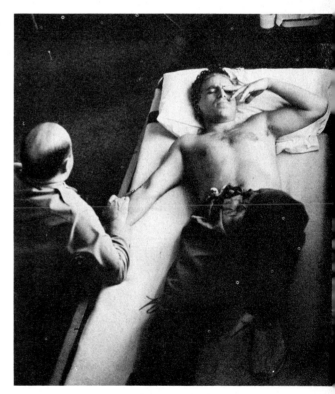

Startling new techniques in psychotherapy are
developed for "war fatigued" G.I.'s. Sodium amytal
injected into a vein promotes "narcosynthesis."
Losing their inhibitions they pour out streams
of talk. The doctor is now able to get
to the focal point of anxiety quickly.

to the annals of the nation. As an example 11,700 new students entered Harvard in 1946, three-quarters of them veterans. Schools were jammed.

The returning GI's, if they were not bored by politics, had a lot to look at in Washington. Mr. Truman was beginning to show his colors. Sometimes he was inept, sometimes hasty, and sometimes far too generous to old favorites or new associates. But he had at least two qualities that nobody could easily deny—courage and his belief in the fundamental decency of man. He was fully aware of his own limitations, but his optimism was unflagging and he was packed with guts. The historians will probably give him higher rank as a President than he seemed to have at the time.

The air age is upon us. In Chattanooga a 7-year-old public school student learns about aviation in simulated cockpit.

Flying Wing experimental bomber (weight 104 tons) undergoes first test.

Schools become crowded to suffocation. Children in foreground are newcomers, must be absorbed into primary school (at Artesia, near Los Angeles) already jammed. Classes operate in two shifts.

Steaks cost $1.35 a pound on the black market, if you could get them, and if it had not been for controls rents would have gone out of sight. But inflation at home was only one of several vexing problems confronting the new President. He made Averell Harriman Ambassador to Great Britain and then brought him home to be Secretary of Commerce. Henry Wallace was ousted from the Cabinet because of a policy disagreement about Russia. The inordinately complex and important problem of atomic energy was dumped on a President's lap for the first time. And there was much else. Mr. Truman set about merging the armed forces into a single Department of Defense, vetoed the Case (anti-strike) Bill, and in general did what he could to protect the interests of the so-called "little" man, particularly after most price controls were lifted.

1946 was not only the year of the first big bomb tests at Bikini (over and under water) but of such crazinesses in the national scene as a marriage ceremony performed by a three-year-old boy, who had been ordained as a "pastor" by a California crackpot sect. It was the year in which Harry Hopkins died, and also Gertrude Stein. An airplane crashed into the Bank of Manhattan Building in New York City, and a jet-propelled plane set a non-stop record by flying *across the US* in four hours, thirteen minutes, twenty-six seconds. People read a book about the Madison Avenue mind called "The Hucksters," and in Boston the censors cut the expression "Oh, God" from the Crouse-Lindsay play "Life With Father." The Philippines became independent. The Chemical Warfare Service announced the development of a poison so powerful that one ounce would kill the entire population of the United States, and during the year the country spent $8 billion on alcoholic drinks.

Just too late, after hours in line, to buy a pork chop. Meat shortage irritates the nation.

In newly crowded California two girls start building a home out of plane fuselage.

Puerto Ricans flock to the East Coast. Family of 10 squeezes into 2½ rooms in Harlem.

We had plenty to think about at home; domestic problems were pressing and copious enough. But while we sought to concentrate on these, we found that, in a sense, the war was still not over. Reluctantly we had to spend more time and energy in a ceaseless scrutiny of events abroad.

(1) The UN started to function, in spite of continuing and repeated Russian vetoes. (2) The old colonial system began to break up, and American influence spread in the Middle East. India, Indonesia, Egypt, and other states in Asia and Africa, on the brink of freedom, strove to be fully free. Mr. Truman did his best, against strong British objections, to work out a solution for the tragic dilemma in Palestine. (3) The beginnings of collapse in China came—not because Chiang Kai-shek was "betrayed" by the State Department, but, most responsible people think, because Chiang's China was too feeble, selfishly run, and corrupt to maintain military strength. This is not to say that the State Department may not have pursued unwise policies.

It would be difficult to determine when, in terms of an exact day, the Cold War began. There were wrangles between the United States and the Soviet

U.S. history is written abroad as well as home. G.I.'s and Russian troops meet for first time on Elbe. Their eager handshakes seem a mockery now.

Union over Manchuria, Germany, Greece, Iran, and atomic energy. In Paris, Secretary of State Byrnes and the Western Allies did their best to write peace treaties for the minor powers, while the Russians steadily consolidated their position in eastern Europe. And the truce patched up in China by General Marshall was rudely broken. Stalin announced that any talk of a new war was "ridiculous" and the Soviets claimed that their obstructionist policy was "defensive," but they broke agreement

after agreement,

while stalling for time and trying to counteract our possession of the bomb. As the Russians saw it, the United States was the "warmonger." It soon became clear that the allied coalition had broken up. A new and possibly catastrophic situation forced itself on the world, and was to dominate practically all political developments in the entire decade. The US and the USSR, each heading an immense bloc, not only competed for world leadership; two hostile and mutually antipathetic ways of life met face to face.

Smiling Communist leader Mao Tse-tung is toasted by Generalissimo Chiang Kai-shek, in celebration of China's V-J Day. The smiles did not last long.

Oil strikes in Arabia transform barren desert, and extend the American frontier. Arab youngsters learn U.S. games.

Mr. Truman greets Prime Minister Attlee in Washington. Foreign policy differences and atomic energy control were discussed.

It's a world on wheels. Kids in California like hopped-up jalopies.

America goes ballet crazy. Two ballerinas practice on railway tracks while doing one-night stands in Iowa.

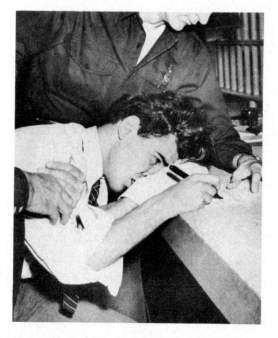

17-year-old "model youth" William Heirens committed one of decade's most gruesome, neurotic crimes—kidnapping and murder of Degnan child.

We had fun, though. We had lots of fun. Gas rationing became a thing of the past, and spectator sports reached unprecedented audiences. Some children sought expression, unfortunately enough, in fields far removed from sport, and juvenile delinquency—a forerunner of teen-age gangsterism later —began to worry parents, teachers, and the courts.

Domestic politics

kept right on going.

The Truman administration, which did not seem to have an adhesive enough hold on affairs, faced angry trouble on several fronts. The Republicans won the mid-term elections (1946), and gained control of both houses of Congress. Senator Fulbright of Arkansas—who made a signal contribution to the decade by the scholarships named for him—found this so dismaying that he suggested that Mr. Truman should resign the presidency in favor of some Republican, in order to keep government functioning. He did not know Mr. Truman.

Among the new Republican faces in Washington was that of Senator Joseph R. McCarthy, who had been a Democrat not long before.

Texas booms. Jewelry salesman sells
his wares to millionaire
in an oil field.

36-year-old Wisconsin unknown, Joe McCarthy,
capitalized on war record,
beat "Bob" LaFollette for Senate.
To be continued.

Jackie Robinson, first Negro in major league baseball.

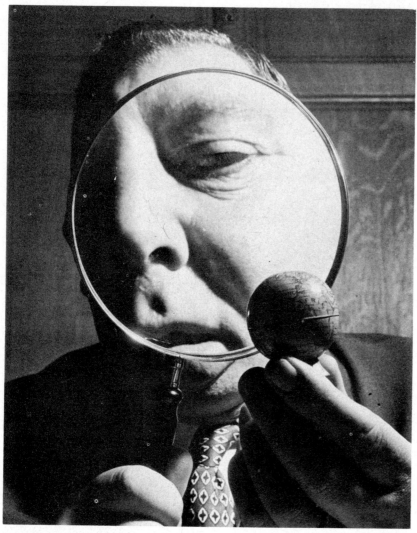

Trygve Lie of UN looks at a small world through a big magnifying glass. Indeed, the world is shrinking.

Arriving for UN meeting, Manuilsky, Vishinsky, and Molotov take a not too carefree walk on the "Queen Elizabeth."

Winston Churchill, superb coiner of phrases, never coined one more pregnant than "Iron Curtain," speaking at Fulton, Missouri, March, 1946.

Not all of us could visualize the map. Mr. Churchill, with his incomparable ability to foresee and seize issues and state them in challenging terms, spelled out the new frontiers for us. He shared a platform with President Truman at Fulton, Missouri, and told the world that an "Iron Curtain" had "descended across the Continent" from the Baltic to Trieste. He asked for a firm "fraternal association" between the United States and Great Britain, and said that it would be "criminal madness" to give the atom bomb secret away. (Little did anybody know that the Russians were already a long way toward having it.)

Mr. Churchill's speech shocked some people here and abroad, because they thought that it was too bellicose. Pearl Buck said, "We are nearer war

tonight than last night." George Bernard Shaw (he was still alive) agreed.

The speech, like so many of Mr. Churchill's, marked a

genuine turning point.

We could not stick our heads in the sand and pretend any longer that we had not been warned. Mr. Truman said, "We are either headed for complete destruction or facing the greatest age in history."

Echoes of the last war still sounded. Ten top Nazis were hanged, as were the malodorous Japanese generals Yamashita and Homma, leader of the death march on Bataan. Some people had presumably been taught a lesson.

Bernard Baruch and Andrei Gromyko
watch fight at Yankee Stadium.
Atomic fight was stiffer.

In West Virginia two of Lewis's men walk along railway, enjoying "no-day work week."

John L. Lewis feels fine. His miners take "sick leave" from work, but do not break law by going on formal strike.

Meantime, at home, labor took a good share of the news. **1946** was a big year for strikes. Industry was expanding at a prodigious rate, and output reached an unprecedented level. The nation was producing goods worth $150 billion a year. Naturally labor wanted a fair stake in this bonanza, particularly since prices continued to rise crazily. The prewar dollar was now worth 69¢, and a man's white shirt—if you could find one—might cost $10.

On January 20 (1946), eight hundred thousand steelworkers dropped their tools in what was called "the greatest strike in history," tying up 1,202 companies in 30 states. Philip Murray, head of the United Steelworkers, one of the best run and most adult unions in the country, asked for a pay raise of 25¢ an hour, but Big Steel refused to pay more than 15¢. The government suggested 18½¢, which is what the workers finally got, when the strike ended in mid-February. The whole issue was mixed up with OPA (which was still in force as of that date), since the industry insisted that it could not afford to pay higher wages unless it was allowed to raise prices correspondingly.

The United Auto Workers, CIO, biggest union in the world—it had 1,125,-000 members during the war—launched a strike at General Motors that lasted 113 days, and was settled at last on the same terms as the steel strike—increase in workers' pay of 18½¢ per hour. In sharp contrast to previous strikes in the Detroit area, there was no bloodshed or disorder—

not a single bloody nose.

The good statesmanship of Walter Reuther, who became president of the UAW for the first time in 1946, was largely responsible for this on the labor side. Meantime Reuther vigorously squelched Communists and extreme left-wingers within his own organization. They continued to make trouble for a time, but Reuther stayed on top.

John L. Lewis made vigorous news all year. His coal miners went on strike twice, with 400,000 men quitting work. Dim-outs and "brown-outs" went into force all over the country to save fuel, and railway service was curtailed. Lewis refused to obey a federal order to call off the second strike; as a result the United Mine Workers were fined $3,500,000 and Lewis himself was fined $10,000 by a federal court. The UMW, needless to say, did not lose faith in Lewis, and in fact—some time later—it raised his salary neatly from $25,000 to $50,000 a year.

Woman passenger manages to squeeze through window of one of last trains to leave New York, as railway strike threatens.

Costumers and Make-Up Artists Union both claim right to make falsies. Arbitration gave cloth falsies to former, rubber to latter.

Underpaid schoolteachers strike in St. Paul, Minn., and call attention to a national problem.

One way in which the average citizen took the load off, during this year of acute strain and readjustment, was with sport. Among baseball heroes were Bob Feller, who pitched 348 strikeouts, and Hank Greenberg, who led both leagues in home runs. Jack Kramer, recently discharged from the Coast Guard, won the national tennis singles, and Lloyd Mangrum, an ex-GI, did notably in golf. Army and Notre Dame played a sensational but anticlimactic zero-zero tie.

And we took the load off with

entertainment too.

"The Voice of the Turtle," "Harvey," and "Carousel" were still playing on Broadway. "The Iceman Cometh," the first play by Eugene O'Neill to reach Broadway in thirteen years, proved once more that the most profound of American playwrights had not lost his magic if neurotic touch. Two new comedies, "Born Yesterday" by Garson Kanin and "State of the Union" by Russel Crouse and Howard Lindsay, treated political themes with deft sophistication. The greatest performance of the year was beyond doubt that of Laurence Olivier in "Oedipus," brought to the United States by the Old Vic. His groans still ring.

Some otherwise sane citizens like marathon dancing. Contestant is ruled out when both knees touch floor.

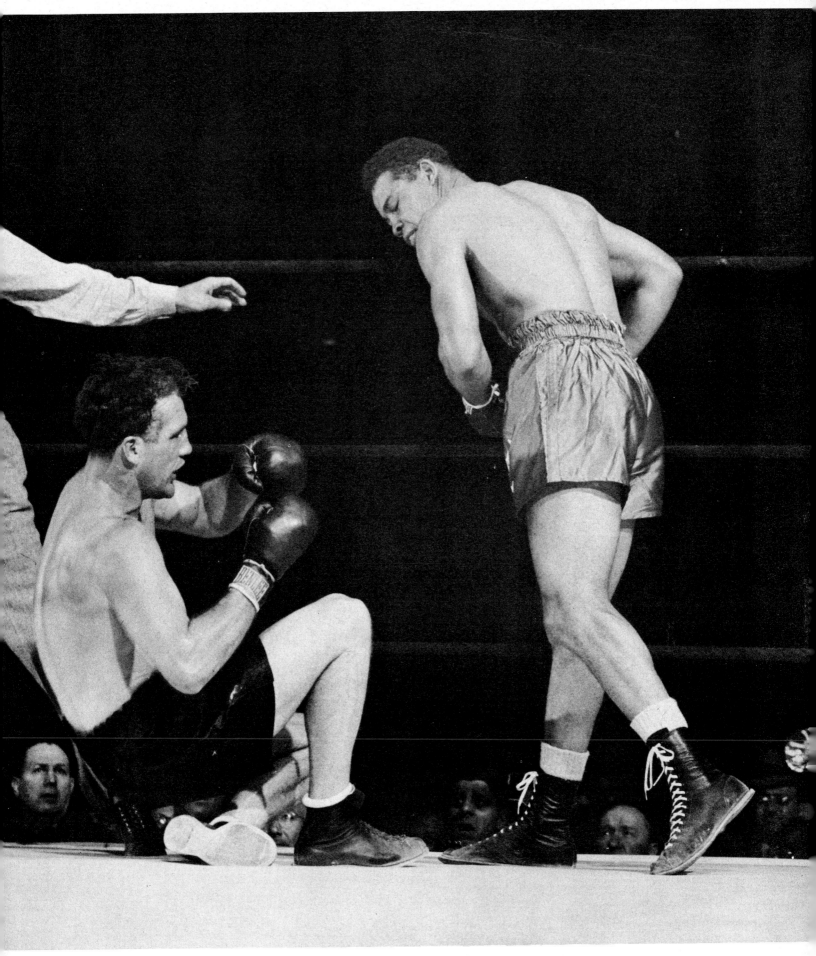

The immortal and incomparable Joe Louis,
World's Heavyweight Champion for more than eleven years,
knocks out Billy Conn. Louis's purse: $625,916.

...ta Hayworth, most flamboyant of movie
...eauties in first years of the decade,
...ore a gown in "Gilda" that gave enticing
...otice of breastline styles to come.

"The Lost Weekend" brilliantly brought
problem of alcoholism to the screen—
with a harrowing performance
by Ray Milland.

Among movies "The Best Years of Our Lives" was outstanding, and other entertaining films, for varying reasons, were "The Razor's Edge," "Anna and the King of Siam," and "The Kid from Brooklyn," with Danny Kaye.

The year brought some

hard knocks to radio,

and few new talents rose. Veterans like Fred Allen and Walter Winchell still led the field, and the incomparable "Information Please" was still with us. The FCC complained—but not in relation to these—of "a serious deterioration in broadcast standards," and a lot of people took a dim view of the kind of commercials thrust down our clogged ears.

Politics occupied almost everybody. Various Republican heads—Dewey, Bricker, Stassen, Taft, Warren—could be seen on the horizon, and they were all looking perkily two years ahead, to 1948. MacArthur too was spoken of as a possible candidate, at least by MacArthur followers. People thought blithely that anybody, absolutely anybody, could beat Truman, and that the Republican nomination would be tantamount to election. The Democrats were being riven by scandal, and Truman's prestige was low.

At about this time General Eisenhower, totally against his will, began to be injected into the political scene. As Chief of Staff, i.e., head of the Army,

Bob Hope and Bing Crosby walked, danced, sang, and laughed their way around the world and into hearts of millions of fans.

Written by Robert E. Sherwood and directed by William Wyler, "The Best Years of Our Lives" reflected postwar problems of readjustment in an adult and magnificently acted picture.

Boss Crump of Memphis, Tennessee,
soon to die discredited,
here rides high, still controls city's
vote by a mixture of polite terrorism
and giving favors.

he was outside politics, and rightly so. But he was also incomparably the most popular living American, and movements to draft him for the presidency were inevitable. He worked in close harmony with President Truman, and Democrats as well as Republicans began to think of the irresistible power, glamour, and attraction of his name. But Eisenhower abhorred politics. He was busy at his job in the Pentagon. He wanted to complete the giant and intricate process of demobilization, see that unification of the armed services progressed smoothly, and prepare the way for universal military service. Also he kept his eye on things abroad, because—then as now—what he cared about most in the world was peace. He was the most widely traveled Chief of Staff in US history, and visited during his term Canada, Japan, China, Mexico, Brazil, and Europe. Somebody asked him about the "Draft Ike" movement. His reply was, "Don't bring up

that damnable subject

of politics in which I have no damned interest." But the very irritation and vigor with which he said this probably indicated that the subject had become real as well as perplexing and that he had to face it.

Congressman Andrew J. May (Ky.) attends a Garsson family wedding party. May was subsequently convicted for corruption, as result of Garsson scandals.

The "Draft Ike" movement gets under way, but at this time (December, 1946) nobody knew for sure whether the Ge— was a Republican or Democrat.

Ladies of the Chevy Chase Women's Club assemble in honor of Mrs. Harry Truman, may look innocent but know well their political power and how to use it.

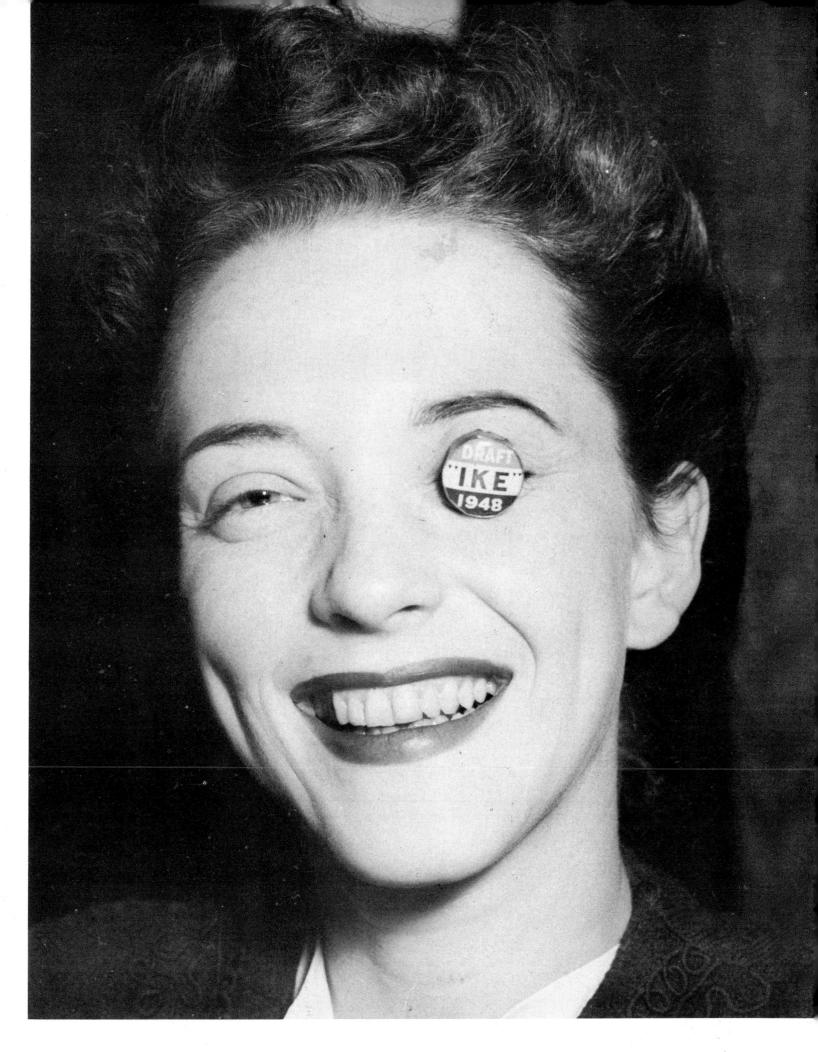

Now **1947** took over from **1946**. For unnumbered thousands of women this was the year when that noteworthy phenomenon the

New Look

appeared. The estimable M. Christian Dior, obeying mysterious imperatives in Paris, decided that skirts should be longer, and within a few months the reverberations of this startling edict were apparent on almost every Main Street in America. Women with bad legs were pleased; women with good legs didn't mind so much. What the men thought mattered little. Husbands all over the nation, whether they liked it or not, found themselves spending money to reconstruct wardrobes shattered by the Dior decree. Women, as is notorious, dominate most financial patterns in the United States. It may be the husbands who earn the money, but it is the wives who determine—to a large degree anyway—how it is spent.

Americans, despite prosperity, thought that they had a great many things to complain about. One was taxes. Twice Congress passed a bill for income tax reduction, and Truman vetoed it each time. One was labor. The Taft-Hartley Act went into effect, the first law since the New Deal to step on labor's toes. Truman vetoed it, but it was passed over his veto after one of the longest filibusters in the Senate's history.

* * *

What else happened in 1947, aside from such grave matters as excitement over the strapless bra? James V. Forrestal became the country's first Secretary of Defense, and Douglas MacArthur, who was doing an impressively good job as SCAP (Supreme Commander Allied Powers), put into operation a new democratic constitution for Japan. William P. Odom broke a record by flying solo around the world in a little more than 73 hours, and

Battle is joined between short skirts and long, representing New Look.

Women in Dallas, Texas, create the Little Below the Knee Club. Motto: "The Alamo fell, but our hemlines will not."

ewly popular
rapless bra gives a big
t to bosoms.

Americans love gargantuan foolishnesses like this.

Frank ("I am the Law") Hague retired as mayor of Jersey City. 28 white boys accused of lynching a Negro in Greenville, South Carolina, were acquitted after a controversial trial which aroused ugly and deep-seated passions. A United States court in Nuremberg sentenced Hitler's personal physician—and six others—to death for having perpetrated atrocious medical experiments on human beings.

Meantime we amused ourselves with fads and fancies, which are big business. People in the United States spend $320,000,000 on amateur photography in an average year. Skiing boomed wherever there was snow, and countless mountaintops were hung with ski tows for people who hated to climb uphill. And we were crazy about

new gadgets

and labor-saving devices. It saved time and served convenience and was fun too to be able to put a nickel in the slot at a subway station and get a cup of coffee. It was only a question of time before we would see large machines in hotel lobbies dispensing ice cubes—thus saving a tip to the bellboy—and self-

A gadget made of tube and blower makes plastic gum bubbles.

Citizens by the million adopt photography as a major hobby.

service carts for carrying baggage at the railway stations. But even the wonders of plastic gum could not blind Americans to some other realities in the contemporary world. One was food, a subject even more vital to housewives than skirtlines. Much of Europe, we learned, faced starvation. Food, prices, and foreign policy became inextricably tangled together because, in order to keep Europe alive, it appeared that we would have to eat less at home, which nobody wanted to do. Mr. Truman asked Congress for $580,000,000 in emergency relief to stave off hunger abroad, and urged meatless Tuesdays and eggless Thursdays for citizens at home. Our children drank more milk and orange juice and ate more ice cream than any people in the history of the world. But in Germany the average food ration was down to 800 calories a day, and in Britain citizens got 20¢ worth of meat a week.

General Eisenhower, hard as he tried, could not keep out of the political news. His tenure as Chief of Staff would be over soon, and neither Republicans nor Democrats would let him alone. In October, 1947, he issued a statement to the effect that he "neither sought nor desired political office." But political office wanted him.

Coffee will come with cream if customer dials right.

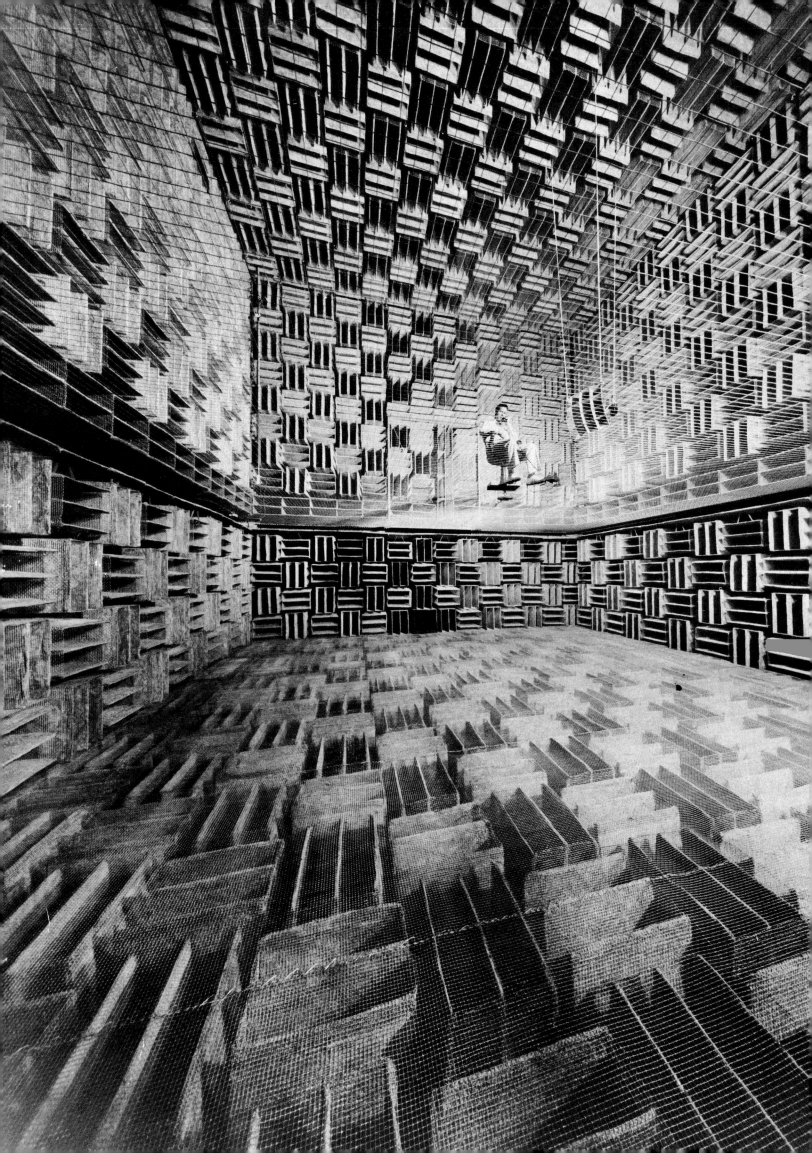

Bell Telephone engineers build one of strangest rooms in world. It eliminates 99.98% of all sound, is used for experiments in checking fidelity of transmission and other instruments.

Strike empties switchboards in a New York exchange usually crammed with calls. Human element in world of communication has not entirely disappeared.

Science, both pure and applied, became a subject that we had to know something about whether we understood it or not. A piloted airplane flew faster than the speed of sound for the first time in **1947**. This may seem commonplace now, but it was sensational then. Meteorological specialists seeded clouds with chemicals, and for the first time produced artificial rain. This seemed to indicate that, in time,

man might learn

how to control the vagaries of something traditionally thought to be one thing in life beyond control—the weather. In New Mexico army engineers, assisted by German scientists, experimented zealously with guided missiles, which might in time turn out to be a new means whereby the world could efficiently destroy itself.

The Atomic Energy Commission, under David Lilienthal, had taken over control of all nuclear activities in the nation, and was now one of the two or three most critical and sensitive of all government departments. Its ramifications became so widespread that it put the government into business, so to speak, on levels not dreamed of before. Mr. Lilienthal gave satisfaction and inspiration to multitudes, when his confirmation was being debated, by surviving attacks from the archaic Senator McKellar of Tennessee and others. The AEC made preparations for new bomb tests at Eniwetok, out in the Pacific. Also it began to work in realms more peaceable, by furnishing invaluable radioactive isotopes to research institutions all over the United States.

Obviously the country needed all the scientific brains it could get. But, as of this date, comparatively few young men wanted to address themselves to a field so rigorous. We were producing plenty of lawyers and football players, but not enough Ph.D.'s. Another difficulty was that the new loyalty-security program began to frighten scientists who were associated with highly secret government projects. What has been aptly called "the agony of the

Search for expert technicians is incessant. G.E. personnel director courts a graduating student.

Actor Bill Boyd (Hopalong Cassidy) had firm, warm place in millions of children's hearts, as did Roy Rogers.

Another character who bade fair to enter contemporary American folklore was children's favorite TV puppet, Howdy Doody.

Baby-sitting student does his homework while "watching" nine children at once. Multiple listening devices are installed throughout veterans' housing project.

scientists" began. Men did not want to go into government service if this meant that they might have to surrender their free minds or be smeared. On one side, it seemed, the United States welcomed scientific research with hungry arms; on the other we created an atmosphere making it difficult for scientists to do dedicated work.

The word "baby-sitting" does not appear in dictionaries of the period. But babies and how to look after them when you went to the movies became a pervasive phenomenon of the decade, caused in part by the housing shortage, the high cost of living, and the fact that servants as a class seemed

to have largely disappeared. Who wanted to be a nurse or housemaid, with industrial wages at an all-time high? And who, among employers, could possibly afford any longer such luxuries as a cook or, more important, an extra room for a servant? Another new factor, which assisted nicely in the production of more and *better babies,* was a continuing epidemic of marriages among college students. Married undergraduates were a conspicuous rarity in the 1920's; in the 1940's they were commonplace.

Eleanor Roosevelt and Ralph Bunche study "anthropologically correct" Negro doll. Even world of children reflects major problems.

Children learn bathroom habits from "potty baby" and similar dolls which wet "correctly" when put on plastic chamber pot or elsewhere.

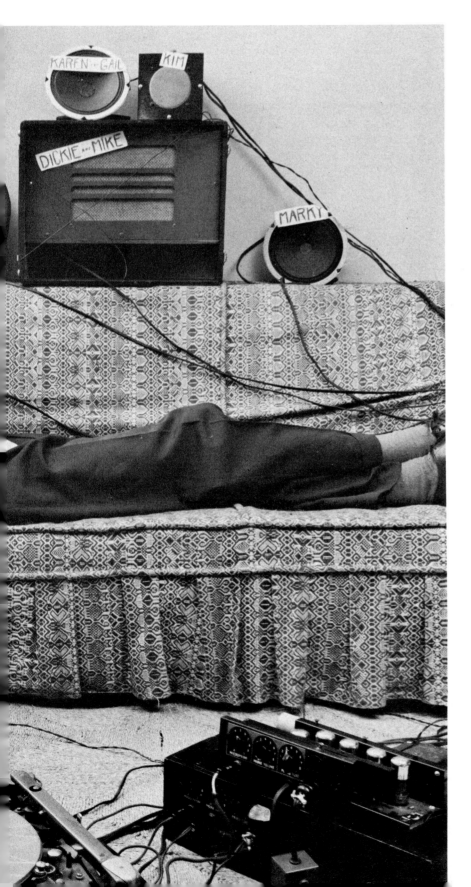

Premiums enormously stimulate packaged cereal and other sales. In one year more than billion dollars' worth of gadgets and gifts were distributed.

Nobody does this better than Andrea Mead, youngest skier ever to make U.S. Olympic team.

John B. Kelly, Jr., 20, wins the Diamond Sculls at Henley-on-Thames, England. His father, also an expert oarsman, was refused permission to enter this event years ago. The senior Kelly, an ex-bricklayer, is now a Philadelphia millionaire, and is father of actress Grace Kelly.

Barbara Ann Scott wins Olympic women's figure skating title at St. Moritz.

A race-inflamed bigot named Bilbo died in **1947**; so did Fiorello H. La Guardia, one of the most spirited and useful of American public servants. Four people committed suicide by jumping off the Empire State Building, and Man o' War, the most famous horse since Bucephalus, died peaceably at the age of 30.

"Finian's Rainbow" and "Brigadoon" opened on Broadway, and people read "Kingsblood Royal," the last good book ever to be written by one of the greatest of American novelists, Sinclair Lewis. Baseball Commissioner Albert B. ("Happy") Chandler exiled Leo Durocher for the season, a Draconian penalty, and the Yankees beat the Dodgers four games to three in a weird World Series. Jackie Robinson, the first Negro in big-league baseball, led the National League in bases stolen, and batted .312. "Babe" Didrikson, the most illustrious female athlete of the age,

performed prodigies

at golf, and Sugar Ray Robinson knocked out Jimmy Doyle. Doyle died some hours later of cerebral hemorrhage—the first death in a championship fight in American boxing history.

Babe Ruth, ailing and overcome by emotion, addresses crowd at Yankee Stadium on Babe Ruth Day, shortly before his death.

World's most wonderful snowstorm paralyzed N.Y., but made it a white fairyland, as 1947 ended.

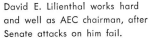

David E. Lilienthal works hard and well as AEC chairman, after Senate attacks on him fail.

Not many Americans thought much about India these days, but India was to become before long incalculably important. It won freedom and became an independent republic (although ties to the Commonwealth remained) in August, 1947. This event symbolized as nothing else the

dawn of a new world

in Asia. Before the decade ran out, ten other Asian and African countries became free. Perplexing new problems in American foreign policy, for which the State Department did not seem altogether equipped, arose. We had been accustomed to deal only with the European powers in the vast areas of the world which were their colonial domains. Now we had to adjust ourselves to dealing with new revolutionary nationalisms.

More than this, India before long became the leader of a so-called neutral bloc. The world, we woke up to find out, was not necessarily divided into halves, but might be split into thirds instead. There were countries, it dawned on our unbelieving eyes, which did not necessarily agree with American policy, which wanted to remain on good terms with Moscow as well as Washington, and which might even, if war came, stay neutral rather than line up on either side. The United States was suddenly put in the position of having to prove itself—before half the population of the world.

Soldiers rake ashes of Mahatma Gandhi, tragically assassinated January 30, 1948.

Four million devout Hindus bathe in the holy Ganges at one spot on a single day. Our Western

world had, as yet, little comprehension of tremendous mass pressure Eastern countries represented.

Greek government, under attack by Communists, might have fallen except for U.S. aid.

Averell Harriman, Democrat, discusses Marshall Plan with Paul Hoffman, Republican. ECA helps to save Europe from blight of Communism.

Late Senator Arthur Vandenberg confers with Secretary of State George C. Marshall as America adopts sensible bipartisan foreign policy.

Two big landmarks in American foreign policy were the Truman Doctrine (aid to Greece and Turkey) and the Marshall Plan, which developed into the European Recovery Program, later to be known as ECA. Congress voted $400 million to help Greece and Turkey stave off the Communist menace. Greece, where a civil war was raging, might well have gone under if the United States had not come to its rescue. Mr. Truman showed exemplary statesmanship in taking the lead in this. The Marshall Plan followed, and American economic aid began to reach western Europe in immense and revivifying quantity. A total expenditure of 17 billion dollars, spread over 4 years, was envisaged. Of course we were not merely saving Europe; we were *saving ourselves.* But there were plenty of Americans who did not understand this at the time. 17 billion dollars is a lot of money, and the country was split wide open on foreign policy. The isolationists among us showed that they had not changed their attitudes much since 1939.

A chief architect of the Marshall Plan was Dean Acheson, Undersecretary of State at the time of its inception. As much as any American, he deserves credit for having helped to save western Europe from Communist advance. It is quaint to recall that, two or three years later, he was to be calumniated by reckless demagogues as a "Communist sympathizer" and even "traitor."

During most of **1947-48** the Cold War got colder, that is, hotter. The Communists entrenched their hold on Hungary, Rumania, Poland, and Bulgaria, but lost a trick when Marshal Tito, in Yugoslavia, broke with the Cominform. Meantime they advanced into Central Europe and won Czechoslovakia, a rich prize industrially and otherwise, by a coup d'état. Jan Masaryk killed himself or was murdered. In France and Italy the local Communist parties seemed to be gaining ominously. Germany, however, was the country where the Western powers and Russia met head on in this race for the Continent, and Germany became the key to almost everything. Continued Soviet obstruction made it impossible to write a German peace treaty, and the Western Allies, convinced that Russia was deliberately attempting to "prolong German demobilization as a prelude to Communist penetration," went ahead on their own. The Russians retaliated by blockading Berlin—i.e., cutting it off from the food and supplies without which, presumably, it could not live. The Americans and Allies countered with the airlift, and succeeded against formidable odds in provisioning Berlin by plane. This was one of the most dramatic and successful episodes of the decade.

But four-power rule over Germany broke down, and irrevocably, irremediably, Germany was split into halves—a disaster for the country, for Europe, and perhaps for the future peace of the world.

The United States, although **1948** was a presidential year and the main preoccupations were domestic, stirred itself vigorously as alarm after alarm came from Europe and also the Far East. Perhaps we had stopped the Communists in western Europe, but not in Asia. Chiang Kai-shek got more than $2 billion in American aid, but this did not keep the Chinese Red Army from advancing. China lay open like a melon. The Communists took Manchuria, swept across North China, spread southward and threatened Nanking.

Airlift, most dramatic of Free World's responses to Soviet aggression, gives succor to strangled Berlin.

Henry Ford, an enigma as well as genius, remained an idiosyncratic independent to the end.

Wait a year for a new car at list price—

or pay through the nose for one slightly "used."

Walter Reuther of UAW recuperates after murderous attack on him by unknown goons.

American foreign policy remained bipartisan—thanks in part to the fore-sight and unselfish patriotism of Senator Arthur Vandenberg of Michigan. Congress voted a two-year peacetime draft for men between 19 and 25, and the strength of the Air Force was raised, after bitter debate, from 55 to 70 air groups. Most important, the seeds of NATO (the North Atlantic Treaty Organization) were born, which revolutionized American foreign policy, committed us to the armed defense of western Europe and parts of the Medi-terranean, and meant that American troops would be stationed overseas for a long, long time to come.

*   *   *

There were more than 40 million automobiles on American roads in **1948**, but these were not enough to satisfy the

insatiable demand.

Cars got more expensive, and styles began to change—cars became longer, had more power, and used more glass. Some new models almost seemed to resemble locomotives with angry open mouths and ill-fitting chromium teeth. The automobile was transforming the face of America, but also America was transforming the face of the automobile.

Traffic jams make congested urban areas a metallic nightmare.
No wonder so many Americans go crazy, particularly
if they drive cars in California.

One technological advance that brought delight to millions was the long-playing record (33⅓ revolutions per minute), perfected by Columbia. These records played up to 45 minutes of music instead of twelve, and you could bang them on the kitchen sink or your wife's head without breaking them. Music, *all kinds of music,* became accessible without bulk, and the new records promptly became a flourishing business. Also in this year TV began to be indissolubly part of the national consciousness, although it was only starting its gigantic march.

On the home front—Communism and politics aside, which will be dealt with presently—our chief preoccupations in **1948** were inflation and the high cost of living. Prices continued to rise, and so did profits, and so did wages to an extent. Standard Oil of New Jersey reported the biggest earnings in its history (more than $260 million), and living costs went up to 171.17 per cent of the 1935-39 average. Food was up 214.1 per cent. Employment

Long-playing records save space, give better music.

Offbeat jazz called bebop has its new kings, like trumpeter Dizzy Gillespie, who knocks fans into a frenzy.

James C. Petrillo, music union boss, banned recordings, later changed his mind.

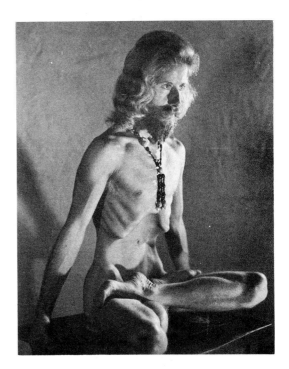

Composer Eden Abhe, author of popular song "Nature Boy," lets his hair and beard grow, relaxes in Yogi fashion.

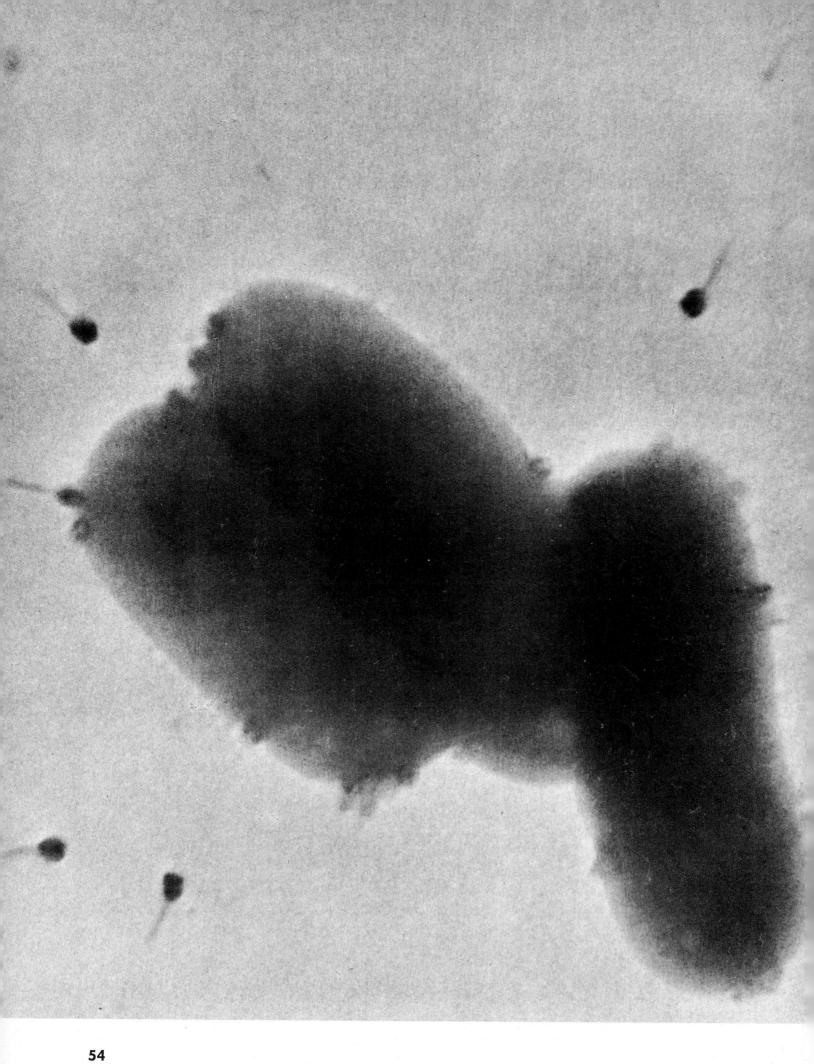

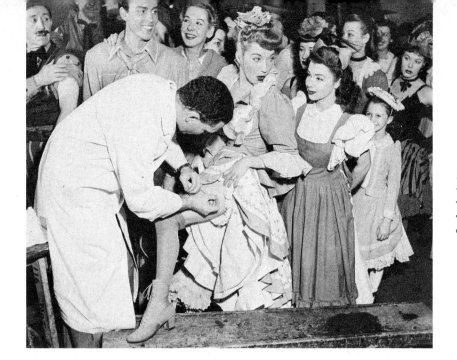

One of first pictures ever taken of a virus attacking and destroying a healthy cell. Electronic magnification is indispensable aid to science.

Smallpox scare in New York forces mass vaccinations. "Oklahoma!" showgirls submit willingly just before curtain goes up.

reached the highest level ever known in the country—61,296,000—but now the dollar only purchased 58 per cent of what it purchased before the war. The more we earned, it seemed (bricklayers in New York got $27 per day), the more things cost. It was all very dizzying.

The United States, thanks to an abundant and multiform diet, unparalleled opportunities for education, and the lively vision of innumerable scientists, was in a position

to be the healthiest

nation in the world. But was it? Were we taking advantage of our opportunities? Did we measure up to our ideals? It was a shock to learn that 72 per cent of all 24- and 25-year-olds called up for Selective Service in the ten largest cities were rejected as unfit. Nearly three out of every four! The highest rejection rate was in New York City—87.5 per cent; the lowest in Los Angeles—37 per cent. What was wrong with the youth of the land? Hundreds and thousands of young men and women, stimulated by advertising slogans and otherwise, strove to be physiologically and cosmetically perfect. No teeth would ever shine as do American teeth, no muscles would ever bulge as do youthful American muscles, no hair would ever have such a lively sheen,

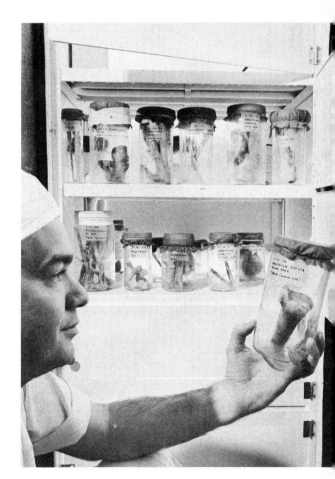

"Bone bank" bones obtained from amputations, etc., are kept sterile at sub-freezing temperatures, and can be subsequently used for grafts on other patients.

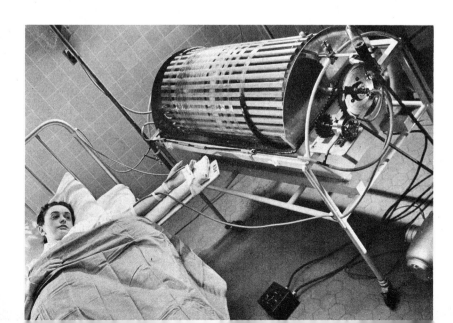

Artificial kidney saves lives of patients. Sick kidneys get "rest" while blood circulating through cellophane tubing, wrapped around a drum, eliminates toxins.

Movie "Human Growth" tells school children about sex in healthy manner.

Dr. Alfred C. Kinsey conducts interview for his celebrated report.

Publicity stunts—made of Florida oranges and bathing beauties—tell about sex, too.

Movie "The Snake Pit" dramatizes shameful conditions in some hospitals.

Insane asylums are not pretty, although they are improving. Public indifference and overcrowding are evils.

no dimples would be so symmetrical, soft, and deep. The fact remained that a great many youthful Americans were in lousy health. One phenomenon alarming to mature citizens was

a formidable increase

in neurotic, psychotic, and allied ailments. We did not like to say so in so many words and we used various circumlocutions to obscure the record but we learned (if we chose to listen to the appalling truth) that one out of every twelve living Americans would, at some time or other in the course of his lifetime, have to undergo treatment for mental illness or outright insanity.

At the same time came tremendous and salutary advances in the conquest of physical diseases, thanks largely to the widespread use of the first antibiotics. Everybody could get unlimited quantities of penicillin now, and you didn't have to keep it refrigerated and it could be injected without pain. Five years before, an earache in a child or an infection in an adult following an accident or an operation could be extremely serious, a matter of life or death. Now such dire illnesses as septicemia all but disappeared, and, to take another example, operations for mastoiditis became virtually unknown. The hearts of parents lifted, and a new era in medicine began.

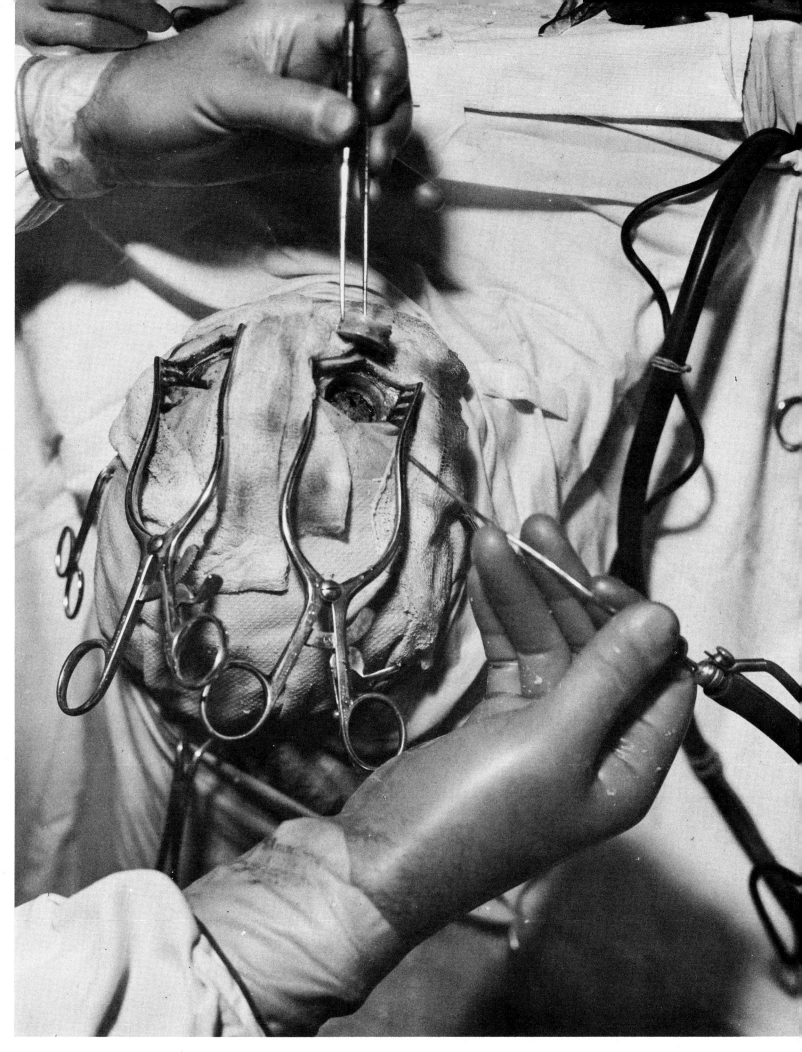

Surgical pre-frontal lobotomy for mental patient cuts off part of brain to release tensions.

Leading U.S. Communists attend rally in Madison Square Garden. In center is William Z. Foster, National Chairman, at right Eugene Dennis, secretary, and Robert Thompson, N.Y. head.

We knew by this time plenty about the overt Communist threat abroad; now we found Communism to be a threat at home as well. To trace the full story of the Communist conspiracy in the United States is, of course, a task for future historians. Here it is difficult to do more than sketch a few highlights.

In the direct political sphere the Communist party in the United States had not the slightest importance. But, we learned, Communist spies and agitators from abroad, working with Communists and fellow travelers at home, had seriously filtered into several important agencies of the US government. Most Americans involved were either disaffected intellectuals with a grudge against society, "idealists" who thought that the Soviet way of life was better than our own, or children of the depression who grew to maturity in the early 1930's, when 14,000,000 unemployed stalked the land and there seemed to be a collapse of all the classic American values. Then came the parade of bitterly disillusioned men and women who, having been Communists, forswore their allegiance to

"the God that failed,"

recanted, became apostates, and sought to be reabsorbed by respectable society, like Elizabeth Bentley, Whittaker Chambers, and many others. It was their duty—and their price of readmission into the sphere of good Americanism—to expose their former Communist associates, sound a general alarm to the public, and tell all they knew.

What they knew, it turned out, was a lot.

The Hiss case, with its fantastic psychological mysteries, brought all this to foaming, stinging climax. But long before the pumpkin papers came to symbolize savagely the conflict between Hiss and Chambers, other events in the same ugly and acid field—Communist subversion—had taken place. The constituted authorities were not unaware of the issues at stake. Back in March, 1947, President Truman ordered a check of 1,900,000 federal employees to see if they had any Communist affiliations. Very few disloyal employees were found, and only eighty-three had to be dismissed. In California the "Hollywood Ten"—writers and directors who refused to testify under oath whether they were Communists—were cited for contempt. Communist leader Gerhard Eisler was arrested, and subsequently jumped bail and skipped out of the country. Two separate investigations of Communism got under way on a national basis, one by the House Un-American Activities Committee in Washington, the other by a federal grand jury in New York. In July, 1948, the United States indicted twelve leading Communists, charg-

Elizabeth Bentley, former Communist spy and agent, testifies about alleged Communist machinations in government departments.

Whittaker Chambers (far rt.) publicly confronts Alger Hiss (lt.) at Thomas Committee session.

ing them with advocating the violent overthrow of the US government. A few days later, Miss Bentley, a confessed agent and spy who had broken with the party, told the House committee that important government officials were fellow travelers, who had given her secrets which she had transmitted to Russian agents. The country seethed. It seethed again when a Russian school-teacher, Madame Kosenkina, jumped from a window in the Soviet consulate in New York, where she had been held prisoner.

Mr. Truman called the Congressional investigation a "red herring," and this caused a reverberating furor. Also the Administration's China policy was under fire. Accusations came that American diplomats were pro-Communist, and had unscrupulously influenced the State Department to abandon Chiang Kai-shek, or give him up for lost. A reply to this was that any diplomat worth his salt had a primary obligation to tell the truth, and maybe Chiang Kai-shek was lost no matter where the responsibility lay.

One irony was that, during all this time, the Communist party had a perfectly legal status under federal law. J. Edgar Hoover, no less, went on

William Remington, named by Miss Bentley, denies her charges. A Dep't of Commerce official, he was convicted of perjury later, murdered in jail by thugs.

59

Marlon Brando and Kim Hunter in smash hit "Streetcar Named Desire" share honors with author Tennessee Williams.

Gian-Carlo Menotti brings new kind of opera to Broadway with his brilliant and challenging "The Medium."

Judith Anderson's unforgettable performance in "Medea" is splendid high spot of the theatrical decade.

record to the effect that it should not be outlawed even though it was a "fifth column." Another irony was that J. Parnell Thomas of New Jersey, the chairman of the House committee, was indicted on a charge of defrauding the government by padding his payroll, and took exactly the same line as many accused Communists by refusing to testify on the grounds of possible self-incrimination. Later the stout Mr. Thomas went to jail. Richard M. Nixon, incidentally, did useful work on the committee at this time, and this helped make him Vice-President four years later.

Hiss, former State Department official and president of the Carnegie Endowment for International Peace, and Chambers, senior editor of "Time" magazine, faced each other before the committee in July, and the federal grand jury indicted Hiss for perjury on December 15. He denied that he had ever been a Communist, denied that he had been Chambers' good friend, and denied that he had passed on to him (for transmission to Russia) copies of State Department documents. Either Chambers or Hiss was a liar. But Hiss, when he came to trial, was not—except technically—being tried for perjury. He was also being tried symbolically for subversion, espionage, and treason to the government and people of the United States.

* * *

And now to happier themes.

Critics said that the **1947-48** theatrical season was the best since the war. In the field of entertainment people were

glad to sit back,

relax, and forget red herrings fancied or real. Aside from "Streetcar Named Desire" the play that gained most critical and popular success was "Mr. Roberts," superbly directed by Joshua Logan. No two plays could have been more unlike. Broadway is an arena notoriously catholic. Two plays by Jean Paul Sartre were imported from France, and American audiences, looking for existentialism, got plenty of 10-20-30 melodrama too. Among musicals were "Make Mine Manhattan" and "Kiss Me Kate," and among distinguished

Movies like "Crossfire" and "Gentleman's Agreement" set a new pattern by their courageous and much-needed attack on anti-Semitism.

comediennes was the imcomparable Miss Lillie, returning to the United States for the first time since the war. "Oklahoma!" closed its majestic run after five years and 2,246 consecutive performances.

Movies had not yet felt the full impact of competition from movies within the home, i.e., television. Even so, it was a bad year for Hollywood. Box-office receipts went down 20 to 30 per cent. "Hamlet" won an Oscar for being the best picture of the year, and so did Laurence Olivier for being Hamlet. In fact "Hamlet" and "The Treasure of Sierra Madre" walked off with half the awards. One well-deserved Oscar went to Walt Disney for a new and brilliant type of nature film, "Seal Island."

In "The Treasure of Sierra Madre," directed by John Huston, actors Tim Holt, Walter Huston, and Humphrey Bogart prove that American cinema can rank with the world's finest.

Hundreds of thousands of Americans found release, excitement, and new horizons in story of Kon-Tiki, balsa raft which carried Thor Heyerdahl and intrepid crew 4,300 miles across Pacific.

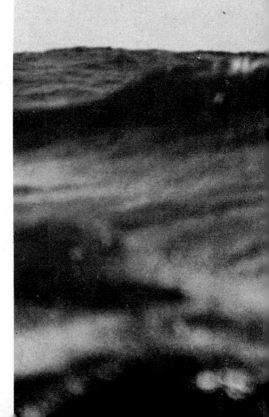

The three best novels of **1948** were, most discerning critics thought, "The Naked and the Dead" by Norman Mailer, "The Ides of March" by Thornton Wilder, and "The Young Lions" by Irwin Shaw. Of course these were vastly outsold by less serious works, the names of which have long since been happily forgotten. The United States is a country that manages to read a fantastic amount of junk every year. Besides we were

in an escapist mood.

But it is interesting to recall that Eisenhower's "Crusade in Europe" sold more than 250,000 copies (exclusive of Book-of-the-Month Club). Anything touched with the magic name Eisenhower had magic. And the first volume of Mr.

62

Citation, with Eddie Arcaro
up, wins 80th running of Belmont Stakes by six lengths.

65-year-old
Mrs. Forrest Burright,
of Maywood Park, Illinois,
raises, trains, and races
trotting horses with
unflagging zeal.

Levi Jackson, star halfback, is first Negro to
become captain of Yale football team, first
Negro to be tapped by a senior society.

Churchill's stalwart and eloquent history of the war ("The Gathering Storm")
did well. Who but Mr. Churchill, having helped signally to win not one but
two world wars, would also turn out to be the best historian of both?

And now sports. *A wonderful colt*
named Citation, from the Calumet Farm stables, won the Kentucky Derby, the
Belmont Stakes, and the Preakness. He was the eighth horse in history to win
all three of these great races, and in all he had 19 wins in 20 starts. As to

baseball, Cleveland beat Boston for the World Series, 4 to 2. The largest crowd in baseball history—86,288—saw the fifth game in Cleveland. But the greatest star of the year was Stan Musial of St. Louis, who led the National League in batting, runs batted in, number of runs, number of hits, and number of doubles and triples, a glittering array of firsts indeed.

The Olympic Games took place for the first time since 1936, and the United States won handily in London after having placed third at St. Moritz. One hero was Harrison Dillard, magnificent Negro hurdler, who won the hundred-meter sprint even though this was not supposed to be his event.

First full-screen television show is presented in a movie theater, shows boxing.

20-ton trailer truck hits a small auto near Indianapolis, squashes it relentlessly into what looks like a crushed tin plate.

The United States is a country so fantastically variegated and multiform that no chronology can give justice to events. Things of burning interest in one part of the country were unknown in another, or produced yawns. In spite of the greatest network of communications ever known, the United States knows surprisingly little about itself in some respects. It is not easy to find out in St. Paul what is going on in New Orleans. Through these years, Americans grappled with a wide variety of local problems. Pennsylvania worried about smoke control in Pittsburgh (a problem nicely conquered by St. Louis), and California worried about smog in Los Angeles. Arizona was preoccupied by the price of water, and Maine by the value of its potato crop. Texas thought about oil, and Illinois wondered if a clean-up mayor could possibly clean up the Augean stables of Chicago politics.

One social problem was nation-wide, the continuing

mass slaughter

of worst disasters of decade—
aboard a freighter
ed at Texas City, Texas,
o chemical plant and oil
sions on shore.
died.

on the roads. Several states at this time did not even make driving licenses compulsory. In the country as a whole automobiles killed 30,000 people in 1948, and 36,772 citizens were arrested for drunken driving.

Henry Wallace, former Vice-President, and fellow traveler Vito Marcantonio greet one another on election eve, New York City, 1948.

End of a third party: Norman Thomas, in his sixth run as Socialist candidate for President, talks to workers in Bridgeport, Conn.

Politically the most sensational event of **1948** was, of course, Mr. Truman's astonishing victory in the presidential election. No one who sat through that November night, with the returns slowly seeping in and bringing their incredible burden of news, is likely to forget it.

But many of us may have forgotten events early in the year. For instance it is striking to recall that General Eisenhower could have had the 1948 nomination—from either party—for the asking. How different would history have been if Eisenhower had been elected President in 1948 instead of 1952? In any case the General put himself out of the race so far as the Republicans were concerned by a forthright letter (January 22) to Leonard V. Finder, publisher of the Manchester, New Hampshire, "Evening Leader," declining to allow his name to be entered as a Republican candidate in the New Hampshire primaries. One paragraph of this letter has considerable interest: "It is my conviction that the necessary and wise subordination of the military to civil power will be best sustained, and our people will have greater confidence that it is so sustained, when lifelong professional soldiers, in the absence of some obvious and overriding reasons, abstain from seeking higher political office."

He added, "In any case, my decision to remove myself completely from the political scene is definite and positive." (Of course the phrase "in the absence of some obvious and overriding reasons" provided a loophole later.) Ike told a friend after he had sent this letter, "I feel as if I've had an abscessed tooth pulled. For the first time in months, I sleep at night."

Even so, people would not let him alone. The General finished his tour as Chief of Staff early in 1948, to be succeeded by the estimable Omar Bradley, and prepared to take over the presidency of Columbia University. The Democratic boom for Eisenhower continued. Mr. Truman was not popular with the Democratic bosses, and besides—everybody assumed—it was not within the bounds of possibility that he could win. They wanted Ike not necessarily because they liked his ideas, because few knew what these were, but because they felt certain

he would be a winner.

Jack Arvey of Chicago and Bill O'Dwyer of New York came out for Eisenhower, and so did several of Franklin D. Roosevelt's sons. It was even suggested that Truman run as vice-presidential candidate under Eisenhower. But the General refused flatly all enticements from the Democrats, and ended the matter by telegraphing Senator Claude Pepper of Florida in July, "No matter on what terms, conditions, or premises . . . I would refuse to accept the nomination."

So, when the conventions met, Truman became the Democratic nominee, with the venerable Alben W. Barkley of Kentucky as his running mate. (Truman had hoped that Supreme Court Justice William O. Douglas would accept the vice-presidential nomination, but Douglas refused.) The Truman-Barkley chances seemed slim indeed, to everybody except Mr. Truman and Mr. Barkley. The Republicans had been out of office for 16 solid years, and the vast majority of voters (so it was confidently asserted) hungered for a change. The big organs of public opinion were almost unanimously Republi-

Tom Dewey, campaigning in Oregon, is greeted by escorts almost frighteningly picturesque—members of Oregon Cavemen Club.

can, and so was big business. The polls showed Truman to be far behind. Moreover the Democrats suffered a severe double defection in their dilapidated ranks. First, Henry Wallace seceded from the fold, and organized the Progressive party. This stood far to the left and had Communist support. Wallace, it seemed, was almost certain to take critically needed votes from Truman in states like New York, where the left-wing American Labor party was strong. Second, die-hard southerners walked out of the Democratic convention, and presently at Birmingham, Alabama, nominated Governor J. Strom Thurmond of South Carolina as the "Dixiecrat" candidate for President. So Truman, in a hopeless position anyway, faced revolts from both left and right. He had to fight not merely against a third party bound to take more votes from him than from the Republicans, but against a fourth as well. No situation quite like this ever occurred before in American history. No President seeking re-election had greater odds against him than Mr. Truman.

Eisenhower becomes President of Columbia U.

Why was part of the Solid South actually splitting off from the Democratic party this time, instead of merely threatening to do so? The main reason was that Truman had fought hard for a civil rights program, including a federal anti-lynching bill, abolition of the poll tax, abolition of Jim Crowism in interstate transportation, and a permanent FEPC.

The Republicans meantime nominated Thomas E. Dewey of New York and Earl Warren of California. There had been some pugnacious primary fights, particularly against Harold Stassen, but Dewey—making his second run for the presidency—could not be stopped.

Truman, however, could not be stopped either, once the campaign got under way. His victory was more a personal than a party victory. Truman put Truman in. This bristly, stubborn little man with unquenchable fighting spirit decided to carry the contest, in person, to the grass roots (which are not grass roots at all these days, for the most part, but asphalt pavements in towns big and small). He made a whistle-stop tour, traveled 31,700 miles, and made 356 speeches—and

to everybody's surprise

thousands upon thousands of earnest citizens came to hear him. His major line was that if the Republicans won they "would soon be giving the farmers and workers the little end of the stick again." He said that the Republican party was the party of privilege, that the common man would lose all the benefits of the New Deal if Dewey were elected, and that he stood for peace (but not appeasement), social well-being, and security. But most of all he won because he said he could win. He gave hope to a hopeless fight. Confidence based on realism paid off.

Truman and Barkley were in fact not merely elected but elected by a substantial margin, and the Democrats regained control of Congress. The Democrats got 28 states, 304 electoral votes, and 24,105,695 popular votes. The Republican popular vote was 21,969,170, but this only gave Dewey-

No wonder Mr. Truman is gleeful. Confounding prophets, he holds up copy of "Chicago Tribune" with crazily inaccurate headline that appeared in early editions.

Margaret Chase Smith, longtime Congresswoman from Maine and one of most discerning of country's legislators, was first Republican woman ever elected to U.S. Senate.

Chicago Daily Tribune HOME

DEWEY DEFEATS TRUMAN

G.O.P. Sweep Indicated in State; Boyle Leads in City

Warren 16 states and 189 electoral votes. Thurmond carried four southern states. Wallace did not carry a single state, but polled something over a million votes. Truman would have carried New York except for Wallace. He did carry great states like California, Texas, Iowa, Minnesota, and Illinois.

It seemed too bad, immediately after this thumping victory, that the Trumans should be penalized by having to move out of 1600 Pennsylvania Avenue. But this was what happened. The White House was so badly in need of repair that it had become a firetrap, and the President and First Lady were forced to shift their residence to Blair House across the street.

Kentucky politico bet on Dewey, pays off by jumping into Ohio River.

And so we enter **1949**, the last year before mid-century. During the course of this agitated year people found—even more than ordinarily—plenty of things to talk about. Accidents made news, and so did crime. There were even crimes, if that is the proper word, on the part of nature. Seldom has any year seen so much bluster by the elements. We suffered stiff jolts from tornadoes in Louisiana, a blizzard in California (San Diego had its first snow in history), floods in Nebraska, an earthquake in Washington and Oregon, more tornadoes in Mississippi, more floods in Texas and Virginia, forest fires in Idaho and Montana, and a major hurricane in Florida. All this should have pointed up the attention of citizens to the need for over-all planning in such realms as reclamation, river control, and the building up and protection of natural resources on the broadest scale. But probably we were more interested in the fate of little Kathy Fiscus. We were unified, as often happens, by "the comradeship of disaster."

And there were multitudinous other things to challenge our attention, on minor or picturesque levels, during 1949. The state of Oklahoma for the fifth time in 42 years beat down an attempt to repeal prohibition. Yes, there are large areas in the United States still dry, at least in theory. The Grand

Taxidriver Hugh Gravitt is quizzed by police after running down and killing Margaret Mitchell, author of "Gone with the Wind."

Baby Kathy Fiscus fell into shaft near San Marino, Calif. Her father prays as rescuers sought vainly to reach her.

Chicago streetcar collides with gasoline truck; 32 were incinerated in the ensuing holocaust.

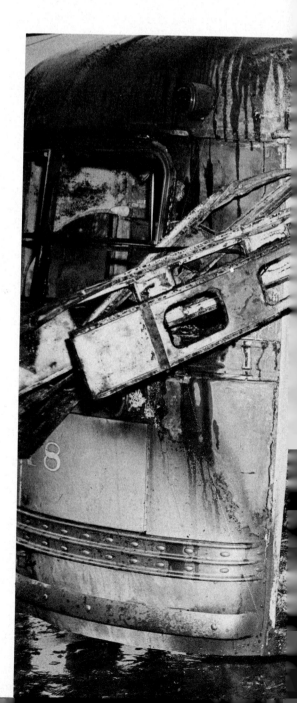

Army of the Republic held its last official meeting in Indianapolis; only six men were present, and their ages ranged from 100 to 108. The Federal Communications Commission tried to stop giveaway radio shows, and we sang songs like "Mule Train" and "Riders in the Sky." Gargantua, the well-known gorilla, died in Miami at the age of 20, and a man sat on a flagpole in Cleveland for 117 days, 2 hours, and 25 minutes.

Other things happened too. The American scene holds much,

not all demented.

Ten million people watched the inauguration of Mr. Truman and Mr. Barkley on television. Cardinal Spellman and Mrs. Roosevelt had a salty little misunderstanding, and the Cardinal made his peace with "the first lady of the world" at Hyde Park. Dean Acheson, son of the Episcopal Bishop of Connecticut, succeeded General Marshall as Secretary of State, and General Eisenhower left his desk at Columbia intermittently to preside over the Joint Chiefs of Staff.

What, meantime, did people in the United States do about the plain ordinary business of living? Materially we had riches at our disposal beyond

Ex-G.I. named Unruh ran amok in Camden, N.J., killed 13 before murderous outburst ended.

New patterns in domestic architecture. Americans learn at last that houses can be beautiful no matter how functional and full of gadgets.

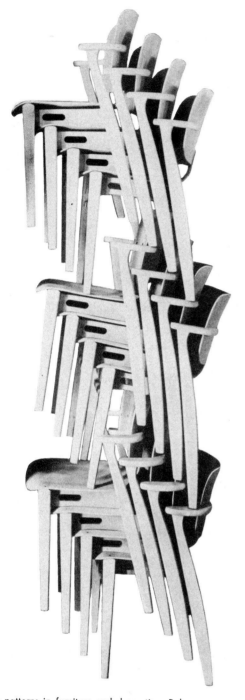

ew patterns in furniture and decoration. Baby
s in outré-looking but comfortable modern
air. Stacked chairs demonstrate
ace-saving simplicity.

New patterns in suburban housing. Huge developments like Levittown on Long Island or this "city" in California are part of contemporary scene.

imagination; we lived at peace (an uneasy peace, true); we were blessed by numberless advantages. But was the country happy? What did we care about aside from a rise in the subway fare or whether or not Rita Hayworth married Aly Khan? (She did.) What were we doing about the amenities of life without which any civilization, no matter how rich, declines to uncouth vulgarity? Did life consist of nothing except eating calories and being on time to work? How much better off, from the point of view of enjoyment of life, were we than, say, a peasant in Brazil?

Well, for one thing, we wanted and got better housing. Styles in domestic architecture began to change, and we became accustomed to such miraculous innovations as radiant heating and the deep-freeze. "Ranch-type" houses were a vogue. New patterns developed in interior decoration—people wanted furniture to be light, compact, and functional. Nobody, it seemed, had room for anything any more, and architects and designers fooled around with drawers and closets and bookcases and kitchens to make them hold more in less space. Suburban communities—the "bedrooms" of the great cities—sought to throw off some of the thralldom of the metropolis. Department stores, to get closer to the customer, moved out into the residential suburbs, and hundreds of communities saw stylish "shopping centers" proliferate. And we saw the rise of the

"*one-class suburb.*"

Rent controls were extended for another year, and a bill to assist public housing and slum clearance passed in Congress after a bitter fight.

And some of us thought about agriculture, since, even if we did not grow food, we had to eat it. The point does not need to be labored that the farmer, who always seems to be growing

too much or too little,

is seldom satisfied with his status. Farmers had in **1949** the second greatest crop in history, which meant that a glut of agricultural produce piled up. Prices fell sharply, and in general the man on the soil got about 10 per cent less for his production than in 1948. And did the farmers yell? They did. But of course agriculture is on some levels a subsidized industry in the United States, and the farmer—in theory at least—is to some extent protected against violent price fluctuations by the government, that is the taxpayer, that is, us.

Meantime, something akin to a revolution was overtaking American agriculture. This, in the words of one expert, entailed "the greater use of more efficient machinery, the better application of chemical fertilizers and insecticides, the introduction of greatly improved strains of seed, and the beginnings of the new industry of 'chemical farming.'" Almost everywhere in the farm belt, mechanization was incessant.

And we were interested in health both public and private. This was the year that cortisone, ACTH (a hormone synthesized from the pituitary glands

Eight combines in line,
growling like elephants, gather
wheat on a mammoth Texas farm.

Friant Dam, part of $400 million irrigation
project, brings water to farmers in arid sector
of California's Central Valley.

Reservoir in N.Y. dries up
following prolonged drought.
Citizens had "waterless" days.

Half million bushels of wheat were stored under government's price support program throughout country. But elsewhere in world, people starved, depended on U.S. aid.

PUT YOURSELF
TO SLEEP

the new way
to relax

HOW
NEVER
TO BE
TIRED

TIME TO SLEEP

Slumber
bath

HOW TO
SLEEP
James Bender

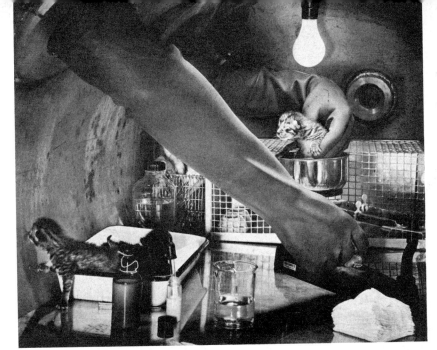

Week-old kittens will be sealed for duration of their lives in sterile chambers to help reveal secrets of aging process in animals.

Among first "wonder drugs" was streptomycin, which effects miraculous cures.

of pigs), and chloromycetin came into preliminary use. It was also the year that the American Medical Association, which operated one of the most puissant lobbies in the country, levied a fee of $25 on its 142,000 members in order to fight to the death the compulsory health insurance plan proposed by the federal government. The AMA won the first round, but the struggle for a comprehensive national health program is still continuing.

Research continued apace—though funds were scant—on scourges like multiple sclerosis, cancer, heart disease, and tuberculosis. A disastrous polio epidemic ravaged the country, with more than 33,000 cases (as against 19,000 the year before). Cortisone gave promise of

miraculous results

in combating rheumatoid arthritis, but it was still costly in the extreme. There were several important advances in the treatment of heart patients, including new surgical techniques and the use of new anti-coagulants. Dr. Selman Waksman of Rutgers University discovered streptomycin—an epochal event— and the application of this and other antibiotics to tuberculosis began with signal effect. The monster that defied the scientists most was cancer. Between 180,000 and 200,000 Americans die of cancer every year, a toll second only to that caused by heart disease. Moreover the incidence of cancer has risen 300 per cent in 35 years, as against a population increase of about 50 per cent.

And we were interested in fashions. The Bikini atoll not only gave its name to experiments in nuclear energy (and already it was being bruited about that the new atomic bombs had destructive power thousands of times greater than the Hiroshima bomb, with hints of even more frightening developments to come) but to a bathing suit. After all "Bikini" connotes

Vitamins are a formidably big business, give "capsuled sunshine" to millions.

"Sleep Shop" in N.Y. sells gadgets to promote sleep. Millions of Americans are insomniacs, and gadgets are better for you than seconal.

Times have changed in Boston.
A pretty girl walks down street
in Bikini bathing suit.

"Which Twin Has the Toni" advertises home permanent wave device, helps build big business.

"exposure" if nothing else. And this was the year when pony-tail haircuts became the rage, and small boys looked particularly fierce in cowboy suits.

As to what *the ladies of fashion* were wearing, "Vogue" wrote: "This year the sweater, its traditional self, yes. This year, as well, the whole effortless air of a sweater—cardigan line, gentle fit, knitted reminders of ribbing, wool jersey—is fashion so sure that it influences tweed, flannel, corduroy." And here is a description of a suit from Paris: "The back curved by a sling of soft folds. Sharp contradiction in the pen-point pockets. Skirt narrow as a pen." One hat is described as "a black felt coal scuttle." Evening dresses were long-waisted, and a fashionable color was "guava red."

Domestic politics contributed a variety of excitements during **1949**, although this was not a big political year. Southern Democrats, supported tacitly by some Republicans, won a long Senate filibuster, which was tied up intricately with the administration's attempt—unsuccessful—to force through a decent civil rights program for Negroes in the South. The Hoover Commission on the Reorganization of the Executive Branch of the Government produced a voluminous report, pointing out how millions upon millions of

One eye is made up, the other isn't. Eye shadow and similar devices make pretty eyes prettier, transform women's idea of what is chic.

Canasta is born and carries all before it.

Mrs. Ralph Smafield of Detroit, Mich., won annual Pillsbury "Bake-off" Contest, worth $50,000. Her championship production—a Water-Rising Nut Twist.

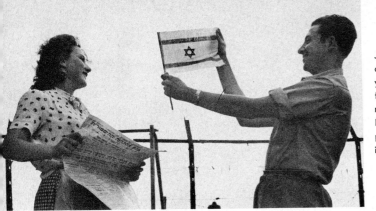

dollars of the taxpayers' money might be saved if we would only make some of our procedures a little more rational. Franklin D. Roosevelt, Jr., won a seat in Congress, in spite of defying Tammany. Herbert H. Lehman beat John Foster Dulles for the Senate, and William O'Dwyer was reelected mayor of New York City. And at about this time people began to hear about

a man in Illinois

named Stevenson. The US has a wonderful instinct for digging deep into the mass of useful, yeasty citizens and picking out unknowns.

Joe McCarthy had not, incidentally, discovered Communism as an issue by this time. But he was getting into the news to a minor extent. He was active in trying to commute the death sentences passed on German SS men responsible for the Malmedy massacre during the war, saying that American army investigators had used "improper" methods. In the light of today such a statement, coming from McCarthy, seems odd indeed. Also McCarthy joined fellow Senators in the useful exposure of "five percenters." Businessmen seeking government contracts passed a handful of deep freezes around, hoping for favors in return.

*   *   *

Internationally we had much to watch. The Soviet Union cast its forty-second veto in the Security Council of the UN. Stalin offered to meet Truman alone for talks on peace, if Mr. Truman would come to Russia. There came a truce between India and Pakistan, and another between the new state of Israel and its angry Arab neighbors. The Greek civil war ended with defeat of the Communists, and the West German Republic came into being, with a tart, strong old man named Konrad Adenauer as Chancellor. But none of these events had importance comparable to what took place in China. Here a fantastic tragedy on a continental scale worked its way toward climax. Chiang Kai-shek's shattered armies, with their morale broken and no will to fight, suffered defeat after defeat, as the Communists in turn took Peiping, Nanking, and Shanghai. In a famous White Paper on China, the State Department announced that it had abandoned hope of being able to save China from the Communists, blamed Chiang Kai-shek's "reactionary clique" for this, and served notice that no further American aid would go to Chiang's government. On September 21 the Communists proclaimed the "People's

Funeral of a pro: Chicago's late Mayor Kelly. Front ro

...ator Paul Douglas; Adlai Stevenson; U.S. Attorney General J. Howard McGrath; Cook County Assessor John Clark.

Republic of China," and in December Chiang set up a government, with what remained of his decimated forces, in Formosa.

No wonder the Russians had let up on the Cold War in Europe. Their allies, the Chinese, had conquered half of Asia—enough booty for a year. The Russians are masters of a kind of diplomatic-military one-two punch. They concentrate on Europe and Asia by turn, depending on which is weaker. And the United States woke up belatedly to discover that a new Communist state had been born in the world, larger than Russia in area, more populous, and with incalculable potential strength and strategic impact—Red China.

But this was not all. Perhaps the most important news of the year was the revelation that the USSR had successfully exploded its first atomic bomb.

Political freshman F. D. Roosevelt, Jr., with his mother, recently voted the "most admired" woman in U.S. He is about to take oath as N. Y. Congressman.

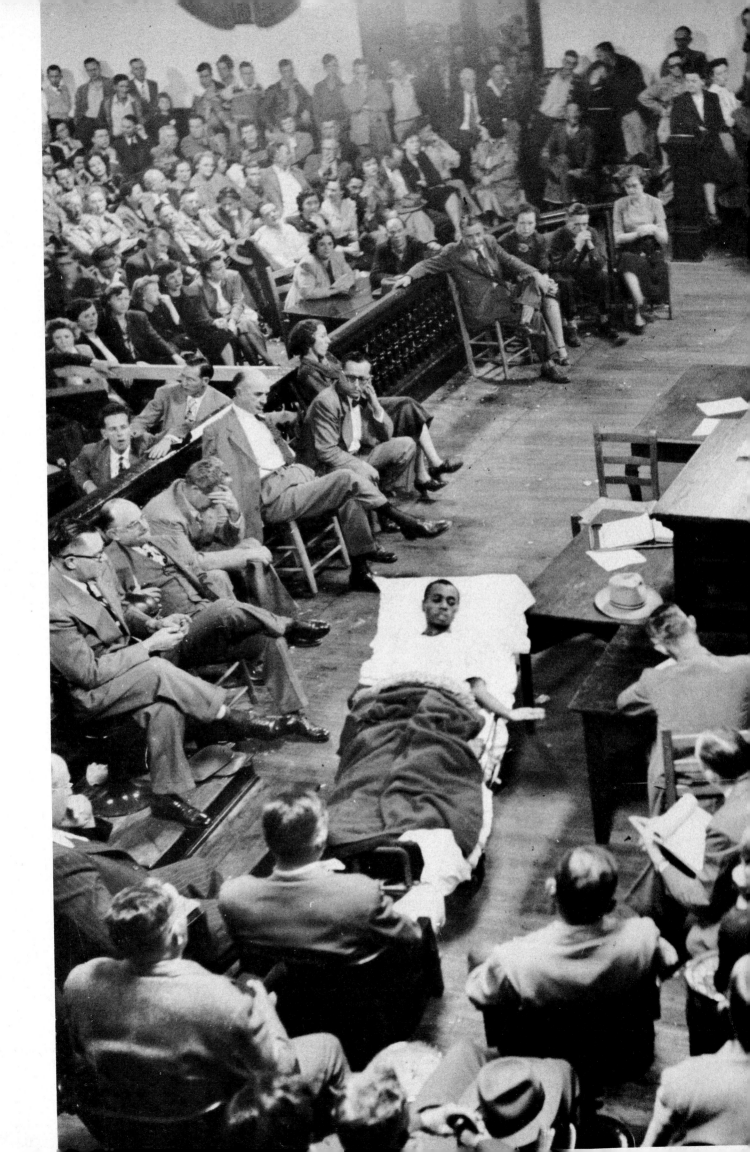

Negro, wounded by shot in spine, testifies against white miscreants who broke into his Mississippi home, wantonly murdered his three children. White men got life sentences.

Millionaire George Armstrong offered fantastically large grant to small military college in Mississippi. College refused to accept because Armstrong stipulated that it would have to stress superiority of whites over other races in teaching.

The United States of America is 10 per cent a black nation, since roughly one out of every ten Americans—man, woman, child—is a Negro. The weight of the Negro problem, the most gravid and harassing of all problems on the domestic scene, was pressing heavily on the American conscience in the middle years of the decade. Atrocious things still happened to Negroes, but on the whole substantial improvement in race relations seemed to be in sight. Segregation patterns were

beginning to loosen up,

everywhere except in the deepest South. More than three-quarters of a million Negroes voted in the South in the 1948 presidential campaign, an unprecedented figure. The "White primary" system was breaking down. Negroes were getting better economic opportunities. Great Negro athletes smashed the anti-Negro taboo in some sports, and, most important, Secretary of Defense Louis Johnson ended segregation in the armed services.

But the Negro problem was, manifestly, far from being "solved." Ameliorations continued to take place, but they did not do away with the basic, underlying situation, which was cancerous.

Negro school children don't have it easy in West Memphis, Ark. Here five grades are jammed into Baptist church, because no other facilities were available.

632 members of prolific DuPont family gather to celebrate 150th anniversary of their arrival in America.

Springfield, Ohio, businessman gives 210 employees free Fords, as part of profit-sharing program.

Women own more U.S. industry shares than men. Wilma Soss likes to sound off against corporations to gain more recognition for the ladies.

"Recession." Line of jobless in Indianapolis wait for unemployment compensation checks.

The business of the United States, according to a familiar maxim, is business, that is, making money. Of course nothing could be further from the truth, at least in the light of most circumstances today. The business of the United States, in a period when individual enterprise has become inextricably wedded to the principle of broad social welfare for the many, is no longer a mere matter of buying cheap and selling dear, exploiting services, or otherwise piling up large fortunes, although it is very pleasant to pile up a large fortune and it is undeniable that, the richer the country is, the more it will have to spend for social services. But the business of the United States far transcends "business" nowadays. The real business of the United States is, in the large sense, to be sure of itself as

a healthy democracy

and as such to be the effective leader of the free world in a period when subtle and dangerous challenges to democracy have undermined the confidence of people in free institutions almost everywhere.

1949 was our worst year since the war in the realm of national economy. Prices dropped, and we found to our consternation that we were in the middle of a nasty little recession, with four million unemployed.

The United States was still incomparably the richest nation in the world, and to many the Truman ideas of a "Welfare State" were "socialistic" nonsense or worse. What need of a Fair Deal, when everybody (so it was said) was being dealt with fairly? Scarcely anybody paid attention to such statistics as that, in what was incomparably the richest country in the world, the average individual income was only $1,436.

Hard words, hard fists, mark activity on New York's turbulent waterfront.

Harry Bridges, West Coast labor leader, called a Communist, testifies before Senate. His longshoreman's union closed Hawaiian ports.

Judith Coplon, alleged Soviet spy,
plans appeal after conviction.
Decision was later reversed.

Judge Harold R. Medina
relaxes after conducting long,
burdensome trial of
eleven leading Communists.

Harry Dexter White, Ass't Sec. of Treasury, frolics.
He died shortly after Senate comm. appearance,
figured posthumously in sensational spy charges.

Alger Hiss, handcuffed to a petty thief, begins serving 5-year sentence for perjury, after most terrific
cause célèbre in recent U.S. history.

Nothing in the decade matched the two Hiss trials for dramatic suspense. The first trial opened before Judge Samuel H. Kaufman on May 31, 1949, and lasted six agonizing weeks. The jury, splitting eight to four for conviction on July 8, was unable to reach a verdict. This meant of course that the whole Dostoevski-like process would have to be gone through again, laboriously and painfully. The competing attorneys in the first trial were almost as picturesque as the principals—Lloyd Paul Stryker for Hiss, with his flamboyant old-style courtroom manner, and U. S. Attorney Thomas F. Murphy, huge, solid, and implacable. Murphy compared Hiss to Judas, Benedict Arnold, and "the devil, Lucifer himself." Stryker, in his opening address, called Chambers "a thief, a liar, a blasphemer, and a moral leper." Murphy admitted that the whole case rested on Chambers' credibility. "If you don't believe Chambers," he told the jury, "we have no case." Yet the incredible Chambers blandly admitted that he had committed perjury before the same grand jury that indicted Hiss for perjury, and had lied on other occasions! (Later the Department of Justice dropped a contemplated perjury case against Chambers.) Nevertheless, what Chambers said in court carried

impressive weight,

and the defense could not break down, in the minds of eight jurors at least, the mounting array of evidence against Hiss. Almost every aspect of the case became wildly controversial. Five jurors said after the trial that they thought Judge Kaufman showed bias in favor of the defendant, and so did members of the Un-American Activities Committee.

The second trial opened on November 18. This time the defense brought in psychiatrists as witnesses and this time the prosecution did not rely so exclusively on Chambers' own credibility. Murphy introduced much new testimony and won his case. Hiss, neat as a fish, proclaimed his innocence to the end, saying that Chambers had performed "forgery by typewriter." But he was found guilty, and sentenced to five years in jail.

Meantime the Judith Coplon case lit fierce fires. Honest and bewildered Americans felt that they were staring into a witch's pot. If a person of Hiss's standing was a traitor, could we trust anybody? We were scared. Who was not a Communist?

secutor Tom Murphy, who later became a judge, stands near celebrated typewriter that helped convict Alger Hiss.

De Sica's "Bicycle Thief" wins New York Critics Award as best foreign film of year.

Our preoccupation with these venomous issues did not keep us, during all this period, from enjoying ourselves in the world of arts, books, and the theater. "South Pacific" opened, and so, at the opposite end of the gamut, did that grimly moving drama of failure and frustration, "Death of a Salesman," by Arthur Miller. The makers of "South Pacific" outdid their redoubtable selves in giving audiences a glowing touch of unconventional romance. And there were

good entertainments

like "Madwoman of Chaillot" and "Detective Story"—if you could get a seat.

Robert Emmet Sherwood won a 1949 Pulitzer prize for his monumental and patiently discerning "Roosevelt and Hopkins." Not many people give up temporarily one branch of literary work, playwrighting, and produce work of equal or even superior merit in another branch totally different—political biography—but Sherwood did it. Another skillful author, John Marquand, added saltily to his reputation with one of his best books, "Point of No Return." Mr. Marquand's basic theme was still conformity. The vogue for religious confessionals continued, and "The Seven Storey Mountain," by Thomas Merton, moved many readers. In a totally different category Al Capp's "Shmoo" set some kind of bizarre record by selling 133,752 copies in three weeks.

Ethel ("Annie Get Your Gun") Merman was still bringing robust delight to Broadway.

With significant and moving "Death of a Salesma

Rodgers-Hammerstein songs give enchanted evenings to multitudes. "South Pacific," with Mary Martin and Ezio Pinza, was greatest musical comedy of decade.

Arthur Miller reaches maturity as dramatic craftsman.

"All the King's Men," from Robert Penn Warren's novel, brings a political story to screen in hard-hitting terms.

What did housewives do, when they were not going to the movies, poring over advertisements that seemed to be bursting with live Jello and cornflakes, and tasting vicarious life by reading gossip columns? They worked.

And they worked

outside the home as well as in. It was at about this time—although it is difficult to pin the date down accurately—that the phenomenon of "two-earner homes" became conspicuous. If only to beat the high cost of living—or maybe because they were bored at home—multitudinous wives got jobs in business. Still another phenomenon was the interest now beginning to be shown by great corporations in the wives of their employees and executives. A man applying for a job was likely to have his wife, as well as his record, carefully scrutinized. Wife no good, man no good—that seemed to be the theory.

Any number of other details about women and their formidable might in the American community could be mentioned—for instance their economic power. Another fact not always appreciated is that women voters outnumber men. It is a wonder, all things considered, that women still had time to address themselves to one of their chief functions—bearing children. But they did, while at the same time some families became passionately addicted to Planned Parenthood.

*   *   *

And this was the year when TV, sweeping all before it, became a national institution. A technological miracle known as the coaxial cable connected the eastern and midwestern networks for the first time, and by

This is what the average American housewife with three children has to do every week. Chores include making 35 beds, cleaning 750 dishes and glasses, washing 400 pieces of silver, cooking 175 pounds of food, and handling 250 articles of laundry. Not included—nursing baby, shopping, taking husband to train, etc.

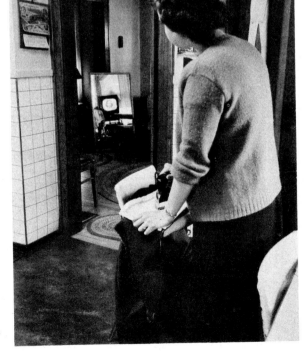

Television invades radio soap-opera territory. Housewife tries watching while she works.

93

Magic of distant sight transforms world of entertainment, and a great new industry grows apace.

December there were 98 TV stations in 57 cities, as against 50 stations in only 29 cities at the beginning of the year. TV sets—partly because of the World Series—were by the end of the year selling at a rate of

100,000 a week,

and the country had something like 3,750,000 in all. This seems a small number now, but it was enormous then. UN sessions were telecast for the first time, under the sponsorship of the Ford Motor Company. The most

Faye Emerson's bosom became almost as famous as Paul Revere's ride or Joe Palooka.

TV even brings outside world to nuns in hospital.

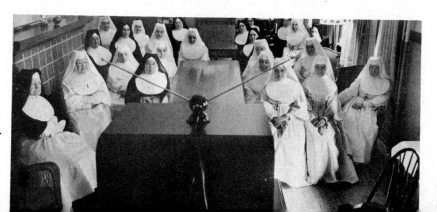

Aerials transform rooflines in thousands of neighborhoods, as TV becomes indispensable to millions.

popular TV performer (for the second year) was Milton Berle; hot on his heels was Arthur Godfrey. TV came into kitchens, hospitals, bars, nunneries, schools, theaters, and insane asylums. There was no stopping it.

Radio, however, was not by any means extinguished. FM helped it among other things. 225 new stations came on the air in 1949, giving the nation 2,800 in all. There were 80 million radio sets in use. A kind of war took place during the year between CBS and NBC, with CBS raiding its rival for high-rating properties. The leading comedian was Jack Benny.

Ed Sullivan, one of decade's biggest TV stars, greets distinguished entertainer Margaret Truman.

Sports fans throng bars, watch baseball. Outdoor world comes indoors.

Aging Joe Louis (36) tries a comeback, and is beaten into stupor by Ezzard Charles.

Sports in several spheres kept fans excited. Notre Dame won its 38th straight game without a defeat, and ended its fourth consecutive unbeaten season. In baseball both pennant races were murderously, crazily,

fascinatingly close

to the last minute of the last breathless hour.

This year wrote finis, to all practical purposes, to the career of one of the greatest prize fighters of all time, Joe Louis. He fought again later, in 1950 and 1951, but never recaptured his former glory. But what an unparalleled, dazzling record Joe left! He defended his title successfully no fewer than twenty-five times, and held the world's heavyweight boxing championship for more than eleven robust years.

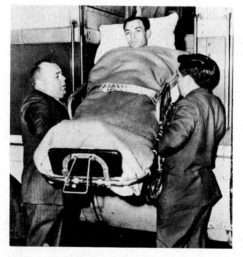

Ben Hogan comes home after crippling auto accident.

Hogan, in contrast to Louis, stages a magnificent comeback, but fails to beat Sam Snead in playoff of Los Angeles Open

ore than twenty million people saw this fight, 22,000 in Yankee Stadium, all the rest by television.

Forlorn sentry sits
on banks of Yangtze
as Chiang Kai-shek's
wavering forces come closer
to final collapse.

Truman and Barkley look on
soberly as Secretary of State
Dean Acheson, imperturbable
despite vilification campaign,
signs North Atlantic Treaty.

Now we must touch on foreign policy again before saying good-by to **1949**. The major preoccupation, in spite of gnawing worry about the Far East, still had to be the protection of western Europe. France (at least as of that moment) meant more to us than China, because if the Russians should penetrate to the Atlantic, the entire strategic situation of the United States would be irremediably changed. We would have lost, in a manner of speaking, World War II. And we would certainly be at a disastrous disadvantage in fighting World War III, if we had to fight it. Already France, the United Kingdom, and the other western European countries had bound themselves

into a protective covenant.

Now the United States joined this covenant, and the North Atlantic Pact was signed in Washington. This marked a truly epochal turn in American policy. Isolationism was no more. We became pledged, as a nation, to "the collective defense and the preservation of peace, security, and freedom in the North Atlantic Community," that is, the Western world. NATO presently came into being, and the contracting parties, including the US, agreed that "an armed attack against one or more of them in Europe or North America should be considered an attack against them all." Twelve nations became members of NATO, and Greece and Turkey entered later.

Economic aid to Europe continued meanwhile, but a refractory Congress kept whittling the amounts down. Mr. Truman asked for $1.1 billion for NATO, and got $505,000,000. The country wanted to defend itself, yes, but at the smallest possible cost. We faced the spectacle of legislators pleading for the stiffest kind of foreign policy on the one hand, while with the other they systematically sought to reduce not only economic and military

Russian airman who defected from Reds joins
Americans in picket line protesting against pro-
Communist "peace" meeting in New York.

Ezra Pound, World War I expatriate. He supported Axis, and is now in Washington, D.C., mental institution. Also he was—and is—a poet of prime rank.

aid to Europe, but the strength of our own domestic military establishment. There were several developments in the realm of national defense. A fierce fight developed over unification of the armed services, and the Navy seemed to think that it was being sabotaged. General Bradley called several admirals "Fancy Dans," and said that they were doing "infinite harm" to the country. Also at this time work began on an immense radar net to cover the United States and Alaska and to be linked with a similar net across Canada. No warning system against air attack had ever existed on such a scale before. Finally in this field, West Germany became a partner in the Marshall Plan and ECA. But it was not yet a member of NATO, and not yet permitted to rearm.

Two other items in foreign policy deserve mention. One was Mr. Truman's inauguration of Point 4, which envisaged American technical assistance to

Ex-G.I.'s and other expatriates flock to Paris, haunt cafés, write poetry, study, and grow beards—even as did "Lost Generation" in 1920's.

Robert Rossellini, who made good films like "Open City," and lovely star Ingrid Bergman fell in love, and she has been an "expatriate" ever since.

underdeveloped areas of the world.

The other had to do with a country about which we still knew very little —Korea. We were to learn a painful lot about Korea before many months passed. What happened now was that the United States decided, after full consideration, to pull its military forces out of southern Korea, and the last American fighting unit left on June 29, 1949.

Meantime, in non-military as well as military fields, many thousands of Americans were *discovering Europe.*

The GI Bill of Rights and the Fulbright scholarships gave a new impetus to study abroad, and Americans haunted cafés and libraries from Rome to Helsinki, from Oxford to Madrid, improving themselves earnestly and learning about European culture, sweethearts, food, and drink.

Expatriate "Lucky" Luciano was deported to Italy. Not since Mussolini has such a mobster stood in Colosseum.

Senator Kefauver quizzes member of Capone Syndicate. Vast TV audiences were shocked, and got unprecedented insight into ways of crime.

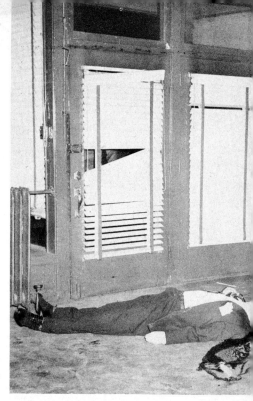

Charlie Binaggio, Kansas City hoodlum-politician, and henchman are murdered in best gangster style in clubhouse under Truman portrait.

And now we reach **1950.** Leading events were the Kefauver investigations into crime and the accusation by Senator McCarthy that the State Department was a nest of Communists. But much else happened. For instance Mr. Truman announced on January 31 that the United States would undertake production of the hydrogen bomb, illimitably more powerful and destructive than the atomic bomb. This was not a warlike gesture. The President said that it was his duty to see to it that the US was capable of defending itself against any possible aggression, and that we would continue to work for the international control of atomic energy. But several scientists sounded grave warnings. Twelve leading physicists joined to say that "no nation has the right to use such a bomb no matter how righteous its cause," and Professor Einstein said that if the H-bomb were ever used, "radioactive poisoning of the atmosphere and hence annihilation of any life on earth has been brought within the range of technical possibilities."

Let us make a potpourri

of other excitements.

Puerto Rican gunmen tried to assassinate Mr. Truman, and a House committee investigating lobbying found that 152 corporations spent more than $32 million in three years in attempts to influence Congressional legislation. The battleship "Missouri," the only active battleship in the American fleet, ran aground, and Dr. Ralph Bunche won the Nobel peace prize for his work as UN mediator in Palestine. The census came and went, and told us that our population was now 150,697,561. Some fancy inventions were patented, since Americans have always been an inveterately ingenious people. One was for luminous bedroom slippers, so that you could find these objects easily in the dark, and others were frozen eggs without shells, slow-melting ice, and paintbrushes that never dried.

Las Vegas, Nevada, gambling capital of the world, has spectacular boom. Picture shows what one casino, with staff of 400, needs to operate for single night. Bags contain $63,000 in silver dollars. Other chips and tokens represent more than $300,000. 29 young women in background served free drinks.

Puerto Rican gunmen attempt to assassinate President Truman at Blair House. Crazy plot miscarried, and gunmen were shot down by alert guards.

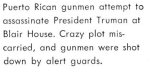

103

Faked photograph purported to show Maryland's Senator Millard Tydings (Dem.) in earnest conversation with Communist leader Earl Browder. It contributed heavily to Tydings' defeat for Senate. "Dirtiest political trick of decade."

Senator McCarthy says State Department harbors Communists, but he hedges on how many.

FBI boss J. Edgar Hoover refuses to turn over secret security files to Senate.

Lee Pressman, labor counsel and former government official, admits that he was a Communist.

Mr. Truman appointed General Eisenhower to be Supreme Commander of the NATO forces in Europe, and General Walter Bedell Smith became head of the newly organized Central Intelligence Agency. Dean Acheson sent John Foster Dulles, his foreign policy advisor, to the Far East to conclude a Japanese peace treaty. Paul Hoffman relinquished command of ECA to become head of the Ford Foundation, which started to scatter millions around like sawdust. Henry L. Stimson died, and so did Al Jolson and Mackenzie King.

On February 8, 1950, Senator Joseph R. McCarthy was relatively inconspicuous on the national scene; a few days later he was famous. He made a speech at Wheeling, West Virginia, charging that 57 card-carrying Communists or men loyal to Communism had jobs in the State Department. Thus began one of the smeariest, dreariest, and ugliest episodes ever to afflict a nation. The great Witch Hunt got under way. The State Department promptly denied McCarthy's allegations, and the Senator reiterated them, although he changed from time to time the exact number of Communists he was supposed to be naming.

The Senate set up a subcommittee of its Foreign Relations Committee, under the chairmanship of Millard Tydings (Dem., Maryland), to investigate. It sat until June and took two million words of testimony. McCarthy, after various evasions and delays, charged that Professor Owen Lattimore of Johns Hopkins University was "the top Soviet agent in the US" and "the chief architect of US Asiatic policy." But Mr. Lattimore was not an official of the State Department. He called McCarthy's charges "moonshine," said that the Senator was a "base and contemptible liar," and denied utterly that he had ever been a Communist or "Soviet agent." Also McCarthy attacked Ambassador-at-Large Philip Jessup. At once General Eisenhower, General Marshall, and other respectable citizens defended Jessup. The whole case became inextricably interwoven with (a) domestic politics, since reactionary Republicans found this a marvelously convenient issue with which to belabor the Democratic administration, and (b) the government's China policy, since puzzled and indignant citizens everywhere wanted to know if anybody in Washington could, in truth, have been responsible for the collapse of Nationalist China, and, if so, to find the villain. The most violent accusations were recklessly thrown about. Another issue was persistent refusal by the administration to release its confidential loyalty files. Rudely McCarthy told the President of the US to "put up or shut up." At the end the Democratic majority of the subcommittee said that McCarthy had failed to prove a single charge, cleared Lattimore and Jessup, and called McCarthy's crusade "a fraud and a hoax perpetrated on the Senate of the US and the American people. . . . perhaps the most nefarious campaign of half-truths and untruths in the history of this republic. For the first time in our history, we have seen the technique of the 'big lie' employed on a sustained basis." The Republican minority members did not sign the report on the ground that "the four month probe was inadequate. and superficial." (Lattimore, as a result of these proceedings, was subsequently indicted for perjury, but years later the government dropped the case.)

What happened in **1950** outside Congress was even more bizarre. Private informers "named" people as Communists or Communist sympathizers, often without proof, with the result that their livelihoods as well as reputations were endangered. A vigilante publication, "Red Channels," accused various individuals in the communications industries of Communist sympathies, and one TV star, Jean Muir, lost her job. No less a person than Anna Rosenberg, who soon became the first woman ever to be Undersecretary of Defense, was accused of Communist associations, in a case clearly resting on mistaken identity, and had to go through the painful nuisance of having to be cleared by the Senate Armed Services Committee. "Guilt by association" imperiled others. It seemed that almost anybody who had ever made enemies in politics or who had taken a liberal line might be accused of being a Communist, and have his character butchered and his life ruined.

No man was safe.

Now, the point must be made with clarity and force that no decent or patriotic American wanted to hold hands with Communists or have them secretly in our midst, and it is incontestable that a handful of Communists and a group of fellow travelers had beyond doubt managed to get into government service, and were dangerous. There was a Communist conspiracy. When an ex-government official, Lee Pressman, admitted in 1950 that he had indeed been a Communist many Americans realized—perhaps for the first time—that Whittaker Chambers had not been wrong, but right. But the number of Communists or officials otherwise disloyal was extremely small. The bedrock of personnel was altogether sound. Seth W. Richardson, chairman of the Loyalty Review Board (a Republican) reported that of 2,800,000 federal employees screened in two years, 10,539 were turned over to the FBI for investigation and only 139 had to be dismissed. And no Communists of any consequence were ever found in the State Department by McCarthy.

Not all Republicans, it should be added, liked McCarthy. His opponents felt that he was an unscrupulous adventurer capitalizing on the Communist issue for his own gain, and that his tactics struck at the heart of democratic decencies in America. Leaders like Duff (Pennsylvania) and Warren (California) denounced his "blanket" charges, and Margaret Chase Smith (Maine) took the lead in drawing up a "Statement of Conscience," deploring "the selfish political exploitation of fear, bigotry, ignorance, and intolerance."

McCarthy, who became country's most controversial figure, takes a nap during a Senate filibuster.

Heads of U.S. armed forces in Pentagon. Left to right, General Collins, Army Chief of Staff; Admiral Denfeld, Navy Chief of Operations; General Bradley, chairman Joint Chiefs; General Vandenberg, Air Force Chief. Bradley called admirals "Fancy Dans" in course of angry unification fight.

We reach Korea now. Important and sensational as were events on the domestic scene, they were far overshadowed by events in the Far East. To the shocked astonishment of the nation, we found ourselves at war. The last war was, to put it mildly, still green in everybody's memory; now, scarcely five years after V-J Day, we had to fight another. And on this occasion we were not fighting Nazis or Japanese; we were fighting Communists. The fact that we had to go to war again (even if the war was technically "undeclared") was disconcerting and unpleasant enough; what was worse, the problem had to be faced that a local war might become a new world war at any moment. World War III was

grimacing in the wings.

On June 25, **1950**, powerful and carefully prepared units of the Communist North Korean Army broke over the frontier at the 38th Parallel and crashed into the territory of the Republic of Korea. The attack, on such a scale, was a complete surprise. Our intelligence both in Washington and at MacArthur's headquarters in Tokyo was caught as flatfooted as were the Americans at Pearl Harbor in 1941. This is the more surprising since tension in Korea had been increasing harshly, and sharp little border incidents occurred and reoccurred. When Mr. Dulles visited Seoul a few days before the outbreak, the atmosphere was crackling. He visited trenches and other defensive installations.

The background to this demands a word of explanation. The Russians entered Korea back in 1945, and occupied the peninsula down to the 38th Parallel. US troops from Okinawa did not arrive until somewhat later, and took over the southern half of the country. The UN set up a Korean Commission to superintend a national election. But efforts to establish a unified Korea failed after years of bitter wrangling. The South Koreans,

John Foster Dulles, Acheson's chief trouble-shooter abroad, inspects South Korean fortification before Communist attack. He looks unhappy; no wonder.

...erican troops left Korea—somewhat prematurely,
it turned out—in 1949, and
...one Korean waves farewell.

Not many Americans were fighting in Korea by July (1950), but mothers saw their sons off at San Diego, and did not like it a bit.

Later American soldiers advanced after retreats, and charged past Communist dead.

Warren Austin, U.S. representative at UN, states Free World's case against flagrant Communist aggression . . .

. . . while Soviet Union's Malik replies stonily. Here swimmers in hotel pool watch him on TV.

under their long-time leader Dr. Syngman Rhee, claimed the whole country. Then Korea above the parallel was transformed into the "People's Republic of North Korea" in May, 1948, and this too—a somber little police state indistinguishable from other Soviet satellites—claimed all of Korea. A few months later, after free and fair elections supervised by UN officials, Dr. Rhee set up the Republic of Korea in the south. The Russians boycotted the elections. All was not ideal in this new little country, but the United States promptly gave it recognition and it had the

moral backing of the UN.

At least a million North Koreans slipped across the parallel to live there. Dr. Rhee and his fledgling government, whatever their failings, were better than Communist oppression. Then the Russians (January, 1949) decided to get out of North Korea bag and baggage. This forced our hand, and the US similarly withdrew military forces from the southern sector, i.e., from Rhee's republic. This is to foreshorten greatly a story gnarled and tangled in the extreme. The upshot was that North and South Korea, two separate

More American and UN troops lose lives as fighting seesaws up and down dreary Korean peninsula.

Marines tensely huddled on landing craft make surprise assault on Inchon, September 15, 1950.

American forces follow up brilliant Inchon victory by

MacArthur was riding high, and few thought when
he flew to Wake Island to meet Truman that
the President would fire him within six months.

entities, faced each other with mounting tension and hostility. But the Russians had left North Korea with a well-knit and well-trained army, whereas South Korea was virtually defenseless, although the US maintained a small military mission there. The reasons why North Korea chose to launch its full-scale attack on South Korea exactly when it did (June 25, 1950) are still obscure. Anyway, it came, and it was an all-out attack indeed.

The United States had no legal obligation of any kind to defend Southern Korea. There were no treaty commitments. Nevertheless Mr. Truman acted at once, when the North Koreans struck. The moral case for immediate American intervention was overwhelming. There was a practical case too. It was that if the United States and the United Nations did not come to the rescue of a small friendly state wantonly and flagrantly attacked by Communist aggressors, the free world would suffer irreparably. The Security Council of the UN met hurriedly, and Mr. Truman ordered US naval and air forces into action. MacArthur was authorized to use ground troops a few days later, and early in July a unified command was established under the United Nations. Meantime Truman ordered the American Seventh Fleet to defend Formosa, and also to see to it that Chiang Kai-shek's forces there did not move against the China mainland. At all costs we wanted to keep the war from spreading.

MacArthur, strangely enough, had never paid much attention to Korea. In five years in Japan he had only spent one day there. At first he minimized the seriousness of the outbreak. Then he promptly and dramatically took over leadership of the allied forces on the peninsula.

The fighting went through several phases. (1) The North Koreans swept everything before them at first, captured Seoul on June 28, and routed the ill-prepared South Koreans, who lost two-thirds of their equipment in a

recapturing Seoul. This entailed bitter infighting. Here marines clean out warehouse district.

week. (2) American reinforcements arrived and by hard and stiff fighting slowed up the North Korean advance. (3) Even so, the Allies were obliged to retreat to the tiny Pusan beachhead, which

they held heroically

despite attack by overwhelming force. (4) MacArthur was author of a surpassingly brilliant "end run"—the amphibious landing at Inchon, far behind the enemy lines, on September 15. (5) Its back broken as a result, the Communist Army beat a precipitous retreat, and we recaptured Seoul on September 26. Now fierce dispute began on the international front. Several UN members, particularly India, thought that our forces had finished their job and duty by wiping Southern Korea clean of the Communist invaders, and that we should not carry the war into North Korea itself by crossing the 38th Parallel.

U.S. bombers attack Yalu bridges, but carefully avoid hitting actual Chinese shoreline.

Thunderbird Division leaves U.S. It made good fighting record later.

Enemy took 3,198 Americans prisoner. Names were released and families in U.S. rejoiced that sons, though suffering, were still alive.

However we swept victoriously ahead, and late in October reached the Manchurian frontier. MacArthur, buoyant and packed with confidence, predicted that enemy

resistance would end

by Thanksgiving, and said that the American Eighth Army could be withdrawn to Japan by Christmas. The war was over—so it seemed.

But (6) a shattering and disastrous new development occurred. Chinese Communists entered the war in force, and, in MacArthur's phrase, it became "an entirely new war." Previously MacArthur had met Mr. Truman at Wake Island—this remarkable conference was an attempt to patch up differences between the President and the General—and had assured him that Chinese intervention was unlikely. But now more than 200,000 tough and expert Chinese troops unexpectedly came to the rescue of the North Koreans and hammered our men back. This was one of the most stinging defeats in American history. A tragic and dangerous retreat was forced on us. MacArthur complained bitterly that he faced a situation "unprecedented in military records," since he was forbidden to attack by air the staging ground of the major enemy. Chinese troop concentrations were massed in their "sanctuary" beyond the Yalu, and immune there while they prepared hostile action. Of course the reason Washington insisted on this prohibition against bombing

One of World War II's greatest fighting generals, Matthew B. Ridgway, takes over in Korea. Gone are days when commanders sit safely miles behind the front.

Chinese Communists attack outnumbered Marine spearhead. Tired rifleman awaits tomorrow.

UN forces take prisoners too. Captured Chinese will be better treated by us than vice versa.

C-124 holds upwards of two hundred men, sitting in double tiers. Reinforcements flew to Korea incessantly.

across the Yalu was, rightly or wrongly, fear that the war would spread to the whole Far East, with Russia supporting China, or even that Russia would seize advantage of what was happening to attack in Europe. Soon the UN forces were beaten back to a line below the parallel again. For a time it seemed that we might have to retreat all the way to Japan, and this was discussed by MacArthur and the Joint Chiefs. But we recovered, counterattacked, and in time—

after weary fighting

—regained much of the ground painfully lost. So a long military stalemate began.

Consternation is too light a word with which to describe the emotions produced by these events at home. And before long the seething controversies between Truman and MacArthur came to an angry head.

But all this, even if American lives depended on the decisions taken, did not count in American hearts in the way that actual day-to-day events on the fighting front counted. We lived with suffering and heroism. American boys were being choked to death, burned, eviscerated, frozen, ground to bits. In April, 1951, the Communists, as the military historians put it in their cold, objective language, "used human wave assaults without respect for loss of life," and our casualties, already onerous, increased. But the last big Red offensive, which came in the month following, was a failure. By this time, as we shall see below, MacArthur had been recalled, and Ridgway and Van Fleet were in charge. The fighting took on aspects of World War I—men lived in trenches, and struggled forward across no man's land inch by inch. The US now had more than 250,000 men in Korea, and members of the British Commonwealth more than 30,000. Many other nations also contributed machines and men. Fierce fighting took place in the air. Squadrons of our Sabrejets battled with the enemy, who were reinforced heavily by Russian-built MIG-15's. Bombing missions by our B-29's resembled those over Germany in World War II, but were even more difficult and dangerous. Gradually American and allied strength prevailed. And on the ground, tremendously assisted by air power, the UN troops forced the Communists into a fruitless war of attrition. One important engagement was the assault on Heartbreak Ridge, north of Yanggu. After thirty-seven days of violent fighting, our men took it. But the cost was high.

Captain James Jabara, 27,
became first jet pilot ace in history,
when he shot down fifth MIG.

Truce talks begin at last. Contemptuous,
indoctrinated North Korean soldier shows
rudely what he thinks of Americans.

16-year-old Maureen ("Little Mo") Connolly of San Diego, Calif., one of most miraculous of decade's tennis players, wins women's singles title.

Picturesque and pugnacious Sugar Ray Robinson retains world's middleweight title by technical knockout of Jake LaMotta.

Princeton's great tailback Dick Kazmaier weeps when he is taken out of last college game.

Giants win pennant after one of maddest weeks in baseball history. Durocher embraces Thomson, author of winning home run in playoff against Dodgers.

Postwar crowds go mad for basketball. Bradley makes point but loses game to St. John's in this spectacular picture.

In **1950-51** came some pleasurable excitements in the world of sport, if, with our thoughts on Korea, we had the heart to watch. The decade had been somewhat disappointing in that few overwhelming masters arose—there were no Dempseys, Tildens, Bobby Joneses, Red Granges, or Ty Cobbs. But it was a delight to see the youthful Miss Connolly hit a forehand drive. Ben Hogan won the US Open (1950). There were two fabulous upsets in football —Purdue beat Notre Dame, and Navy beat Army, ending an Army winning streak of 28 straight games. The venerable Jersey Joe Walcott knocked out Ezzard Charles, and became the oldest heavyweight champion in history.

But baseball provided the noisiest, most

exhilarating spectacle.

With a ninth-inning home run the Giants came from behind to beat the Dodgers in the final seconds of a three-game playoff, and won the National League pennant. Seldom has the blood pressure of the nation risen higher. Then the invincible Yankees, having won their third consecutive American League pennant, crushed the Giants four to two for their third consecutive World Series, but this was almost an anticlimax. In the course of the series, Joe DiMaggio broke no fewer than five world records. During the season Allie Reynolds of the Yankees became the first pitcher in American League history to pitch two no-hit games in a year.

Sport covers a wide and flavorsome gamut in America. We have no space —alas—for fancy dog shows; or for automobile racing; or for the fact that Willie Hoppe was world three-cushion billiard champion uninterruptedly from 1947 to 1951; or for trout fishing; or for chess, bowling or the rodeo. One increasingly popular sport was skindiving, given more scope at this time by the aqualung, an underwater breathing device invented by Captain Cousteau of France.

Eisenhower, startled, hears that MacArthur is dismissed. Ike's comment: "When you put on a uniform, there are certain inhibitions that you accept."

We proceed to other aspects of **1951.** The most dramatic event of the year was Truman's dismissal of MacArthur, together with the General's return to the US and the resultant pyrotechnic hearings in Congress. To understand this fully we must take cognizance of the MacArthur character, as well as the extraordinary position held by the General in Japan. MacArthur had been uninterruptedly out of the United States since May, 1937. Nobody had ever been able to persuade him to come home, even for a brief visit, and consequently he was out of touch to an extent with the United States—with the mood of the home country, its pulse and temperature. Zealous advisers, mostly optimistic yes men, walled him off. Moreover he ruled Japan like a dictator, which indeed he was, and his reputation in Japan was—quite literally—that of a benevolent demigod. It was almost inconceivable to anybody, including MacArthur, that MacArthur could do wrong. All this tended to add flam-

MacArthur, still a hero to millions, receives most triumphant ovation ever given by New

"Old soldiers never die; they just fade away."

York City to a man who has just lost his job.

boyance to his ego, which was, in truth, flamboyant enough already.

Conflict with his superiors in Washington was inevitable on several scores. To begin with, MacArthur did not—except technically—think of them as "superiors." He was accustomed to running his own show, and he had his own fixed and vivid views of Asiatic policy in general and the defense of the United States. He stood for boldness and decision. Nobody has ever accused him of not being a patriot.

Let us go back a bit. First came a dispute over Formosa. The General visited Chiang Kai-shek there on July 31 (1950), and this produced lively speculation and controversy. Mr. Truman sent Averell Harriman to Tokyo to tell MacArthur what was what, since he did not seem to be fully informed about administration policy. This was to avoid formal, full-scale war with China or Russia. But a few weeks later MacArthur issued a statement, in the form of a message to a meeting of the Veterans of Foreign Wars, saying that Formosa was "ideally located for offensive action," and urging a more positive policy. Advance copies of this reached various American publications, an unusual thing to happen, and the administration only heard about it by accident. Truman ordered the General to withdraw his letter, but it leaked out anyway.

Presently, as has just been noted, the MacArthur "win the war" offensive collapsed in the face of Chinese Communist intervention, and relations between Truman and the General became severely strained again. In several interviews and messages MacArthur angrily blamed his defeat on Washington's refusal to let him bomb Manchuria. Mr. Truman issued a directive that military commanders, among other government servants, must clear important statements with Washington before delivering them. Then, after the turn of the year, came two final

provoking incidents.

First, Representative Joseph W. Martin made public a letter from the General stating his desire to use Chinese troops from Formosa in Korea and criticizing diplomats who "fought with words." Second, in what appeared to be flat defiance of the presidential directive about clearing statements with the administration, he announced on his own that he was ready to talk truce terms with the enemy. He did this, moreover, although he had been informed that the President himself was about to open negotiations for a cease-fire. And again he voiced threats to bomb the China mainland.

Dispute over this controversy will go on forever, although few deny that the President had the right to fire the General. The MacArthur case was that Korea was only a small part of a much larger picture. He felt that the Russians would already have entered the war openly if it had suited their purpose to do so, and that the time had come to answer "local" aggression with bolder retaliation. Perhaps a few well-placed bombs might scare the Chinese—and Russians—away. But Truman felt that this estimate could be grievously, tragically wrong. MacArthur had been wrong before.

In any case the President had no choice but to discharge MacArthur. If the United States stands for anything, it is that civilian government must prevail over the military.

119

Burt Lancaster and Deborah Kerr help make Fred Zinnemann's "From Here to Eternity" a first-class film. Innocent movie goer would not know from this still that picture

Newcomer to TV named Dagmar did small spot on NBC show, rose almost overnight from salary of $75 to $1,250 per week.

Movie theaters go dark all over the country, and Hollywood faces its worst slump since 1920's —result of TV, loss of foreign markets, etc.

Turn to quieter fields. Among the movies we saw and liked at about this time were "All About Eve," "An American in Paris," and "The African Queen." José Ferrer and Judy Holliday won Academy Awards, but most leading box-office stars were still splendidly indestructible old-timers, like Gary Cooper, Clark Gable, and Spencer Tracy. Rivalry between

the movies and TV

advanced. A considerable boom came in British films. We began to appreciate the subtlety of artists like Alec Guinness. Some urban exhibitors liked British movies, as well as films from France and Italy, because they were relatively inexpensive; audiences liked them because they were, by and large, so much defter, more sophisticated, and more original than the standard Hollywood product. Soon to arrive were some extraordinarily luminous and beautiful pictures from Japan. Small "art" theaters flourished in the bigger cities. But most of the United States was still depressingly stereotyped in the field of entertainment. If you dropped from the sky into Atlanta, Pocatello, Des Moines, or Albany, the chances were that you would see the same movies playing at the same time, in theaters that looked exactly the same on the same kind of main street between identical hamburger stands and haberdasheries. One of the cardinal characteristics of the US is its uniformity (in some respects) and perhaps this makes a dreary cultural landscape inevitable.

Among news plays were "The King and I" and "Call Me Madam." "Guys and Dolls" was still running triumphantly. Tunes we liked were "Come On-A My House," sung by Rosemary Clooney, and "The Little White Cloud That Cried," sobbed out by Johnnie Ray.

is taken from James Jones's novel about the Army.

"Caine Mutiny," published during movie slump, helped revive stagnant box office when it was later made into a pungent film.

Ava Gardner had widely publicized marriage with Frank Sinatra, set other hearts busily aflame on several continents.

Stern and righteous Senator Tobey of New Hampshire added much to the Kefauver hearings. He was afraid of nothing, and lectured witnesses with wintry sharpness.

Joe Adonis glumly watches hands of big shot gambler and political manipulator Frank Costello, who refused to let his face be televised.

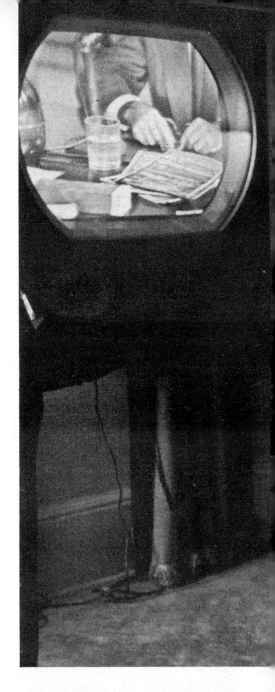

Former Mayor Bill O'Dwyer of New York was a major casualty. He could not, despite his charm and blandness, explain away $10,000 allegedly given him in a red manila envelope.

Estes Kefauver of Tennessee had become, by now, a stunning arrival on the national scene. He was politically skilled, friendly, a good showman, and courageous. He was one of the few men in Congress who did not succumb to hysteria during the McCarthy-State Department imbroglio, and he had courage enough to vote against the McCarran (Internal Security) Act. What first brought him to prominence was a dramatically successful fight against Boss E. H. ("Ed") Crump in Tennessee. He did what nobody believed was politically possible—won a Senate seat against the whole ponderous weight of the Crump machine. This he was able to do not merely because he was an appealing character, wore a coonskin cap, and shook a great many hands, but because he had

the knack of arousing

the citizenry—men and women at large—on a vital issue. Kefauver, sitting in the Senate, began to be interested in crime—how criminal syndicates operated to defraud the public, how organized gangsters influenced politics, and how the country was milked of giant sums every year by the manipulations of gamblers who debauched the police. In May, 1950, Vice-President Barkley made Kefauver chairman of a committee to investigate organized crime in interstate commerce. The committee sat for the next eighteen months, and its functioning became a gaudy carnival indeed.

A formidable array of hoodlums, gamblers, racketeers, gangsters, and politicians passed under the Kefauver scrutiny, and, after a time, under the eye of the television camera as well. For the first time the workings of a Congressional committee were televised before huge national audiences, and many people questioned the constitutionality and propriety of such a proceeding. The illustrious Francisco Castiglia (Frank Costello) refused to let his face be photographed, and the TV sharpshooters had to be content with his hands. Anyway, privacy went out of the window.

The committee took evidence all over the country, and governors of

several states did not emerge with their reputations enhanced. But the climax to the whole bizarre display came in New York, where the chief witnesses were Costello, a young lady named Virginia Hill, and former Mayor O'Dwyer. Millions of citizens, watching by means of the merciless instrument of television, rocked, roared, or became stupefied. And some asked questions that should have been on every tongue. What had happened to public morality in the United States? How was it possible for a miserable hoodlum like Costello, interlocked with other hoodlums, to get judgeships for his cronies, dictate the choice of leaders in Tammany Hall, and, in general, become king of what was virtually an invisible government in New York City and elsewhere, based on terror, crime, and fraud? Why did the people stand for it? What could the ordinary citizen do to break the corrupt alliance between racketeering and politics? And so on—ad nauseam.

As to the unfortunate O'Dwyer, the Kefauver report stated flatly that he

Mrs. T. Lamar Caudle's mink coat became famous. Caudle was Assistant Attorney General in charge of tax prosecutions, accepted favors from people having tax troubles.

123

contributed directly and indirectly "to the growth of organized crime, racketeering, and gangsterism in New York City." Both as mayor of New York and earlier as district attorney of Brooklyn, "neither he nor his appointees took effective action against the top echelons of the gambling, narcotics, waterfront, murder, or bookmaking rackets." He went after petty mobsters and broke up "Murder, Inc.," but never touched the real monarchs of crime like Joe Adonis, Bugsy Siegel, and Charles (Lucky Luciano) Lucania, all of whom were close associates of Costello.

O'Dwyer characterized the charges against him as fantastic, and returned to Mexico City where he was, of all things, the American Ambassador.

Events like these, shocking as they are, should be viewed in perspective. O'Dwyer was the victim of a system, and he symbolized a prevalent attitude to society. Millions of people in the US wanted to gamble, and nothing, it seemed, could keep them from gambling, no matter what. So, inevitably, mechanisms arose whereby gambling was stimulated and protected, and defiance of the law became not merely commonplace but fashionable.

Some miscreants were punished, though. Costello, Adonis, and Frank Erickson, described as the "king" of bookmakers, went to jail. James J. Moran, a principal O'Dwyer henchman, got a five-year term for perjury.

But now we reach violations of the law in a much more dangerous and sinister domain. The story of the atom bomb spies burst on the national consciousness. While Senator McCarthy ranted and stormed, dividing the country but not catching many Communists, the FBI went to work quietly and efficiently. Beginning in May (1950) came a series of arrests—of Harry Gold, David Greenglass, and Julius and Ethel Rosenberg, who was Greenglass' sister. Later came their trials and we learned about one of the

most astonishing

spy rings in history. At Potsdam (1945) Mr. Truman told Stalin that we had perfected and were about to explode a new weapon. Stalin seemed strangely unimpressed. Little did anybody realize that the Russians, even at that date, knew all about the bomb, and were probably just as busy as we were making one. Thanks to fantastic achievements in espionage, they had the bomb secret the whole time!

Much of the story hinges on the person of Dr. Klaus Emil Julius Fuchs. He came of a good German Quaker family. Fuchs fled from Nazi Germany in 1933, and became a British subject. He went to Los Alamos in 1943, and worked in the US for three years. There was little about the bomb that he did not know. At that time security in American bomb projects was handled by the Army. The transfer to civilian authority under the AEC had not taken place. Fuchs had security clearance from the British, and the Americans never dreamed (as of that time) that he was a spy and that the sacred precincts of Los Alamos were penetrated. Back in England in 1946, Fuchs became the chief research physicist at Harwell, the British atomic installation. But the FBI, before long, got on his trail. He was arrested by the British on the basis of FBI information (February, 1950), convicted as a spy, and sentenced to 14 years in jail. He said that he had been giving information to Russia since 1942. His motives were totally "idealistic," and it seems that the only

Harry Gold was courier who got secrets from Los Alamos, delivered them to Russian agents in New York. Now serving 30-year sentence.

German born Klaus Fuchs has been called "spy who did more damage to world than any man in history." British court gave him 14 years.

Ex-sergeant David Greenglass gave Russians details of early atomic bombs, through his sister Ethel Rosenberg. He got 15 years.

Artist's conception of supposedly spyproof atomic center at Los Alamos, N.M.

Two Rosenberg sons visit condemned parents in Sing Sing just before execution.

Ethel and Julius Rosenberg, convicted of war-time espionage, March, 1951, got first death sentences ever imposed for this offense by U.S. civil court. Some sincere idealists joined Communists all over world to protest against sentences. Execution took place in June, 1953, following repeated appeals.

Italian-born Bruno Pontecorvo, top atomic physicist, believed to be in charge of all atomic and H-bomb developments in Soviet Union, was probably even more important than Fuchs in giving Russians bomb secrets. Pontecorvo fled London for Moscow in 1950.

payment he ever got from the Soviets was $280.

Fuchs, in jail, talked to FBI agents, and Gold's arrest followed. Gold, a biochemist, confessed that he had been a Soviet spy for more than a decade, although he had never joined the Communist party. He wanted, he said, "to help the Soviet people." It was to Gold that Fuchs passed over atomic secrets, and Gold in turn transmitted them to other members of the ring. Greenglass, the next man arrested, who had been an army machinist at Los Alamos, also fed material to Gold. He said at his trial, "I felt it was gross negligence on the part of the US not to give Russia the information about the atomic bomb because she was an ally." Then Julius Rosenberg, a former Signal Corps engineer, and his wife, Ethel Greenglass Rosenberg, leaders of the ring, were caught. Meantime, the Soviet spymasters to whom the agents had reported were out of reach. One, Jacob Golos (who had been Miss Bentley's friend and employer), was dead. Another, by name Yakovlev, former Soviet vice-consul in New York, had fled the country.

The Rosenberg trial opened in March, **1951**. Greenglass, who pleaded guilty, gave damaging testimony against his own sister and brother-in-law. The Rosenbergs both pleaded not guilty, and maintained to the last their innocence. The specific charge was

conspiracy to commit

espionage in wartime, and they were convicted and condemned to death. Gold and the others got long prison terms. No civilian in American history had ever been subjected to the death penalty for espionage before, and a great many people, while freely conceding the Rosenbergs' guilt and acknowledging without demur the real peril of the Communist conspiracy, thought that death sentences were unjustified. All over the world vibrant passions were lit, and no less a personage than the Pope urged further consideration of the case. At home came repeated appeals and delays. But in the end (June, 1953) the executions were duly carried out.

In July, **1951,** the most expensive flood in the memory of the country hit eastern Kansas. A million acres of farm land were inundated; nearly 200,000 people had to flee their homes; about 40 died. It might have been thought that disasters like this would make more people embrace the idea of broad, over-all, multi-state control of rivers and their valleys, on the pattern of TVA. The Tennessee Valley no longer has damaging floods. The rivers there are checked and controlled by careful engineering under regional planning. But creation of a similar authority for the Missouri and its wildly charging tributaries was, for a variety of reasons, politically impossible. Meantime, while the rivers stirred and thundered, other areas of the West were choked by drought.

America, if nothing else, is land of contrasts. And it is a land critically subject to caprices of something that even Americans cannot control—the weather. Prolonged drought converts large Arizona areas into cracked crust.

During same period Kansas and nearby states suffered from unprecedented floods. Thirty uninterrupted days of rain made rivers swell up, burst furiously over farms and cities, causing biggest flood damage in U.S. history.

But *the caprices of nature*

did not, except locally, worry Americans much. Even the worst flood becomes a bore in time. We had other urgent problems on the domestic scene. Almost before we realized it, the demands of the Korean War plunged us into a situation startlingly like that of 1941-45. A state of national emergency was proclaimed; Charles E. Wilson of General Electric became Director of Defense Mobilization and Eric Johnston Director of Economic Stabilization. Mr. Truman submitted a record $71.5 billion budget, and the purchasing power of the dollar fell to an all-time low. The government cut the amount of steel available to the automobile industry by 20 per cent, price ceilings went into force again on some commodities, and wages were frozen in some industries. Just like yesterday!

Nevertheless the country was fantastically prosperous. We turned out a record $328 billion worth of goods and services, and the steel industry produced in six- months more than 52,000,000 tons of steel, an amount greater than the production of Great Britain, France, and the USSR combined.

129

Never before had Americans had so much food to eat, although the amount of food that could be bought for $5.00 in 1939 now cost $11.97, and the demand for some articles—particularly meat—

was so insatiable

that shortages began to be conspicuous again, and on the West Coast citizens ate whale steaks. The sales of horsemeat tripled. Incidentally the Army found out—at last—exactly what GI's liked best in the way of food, after conscientious investigation. Four hundred foods were tested. The winner was banana cream pie, with turkey, milk, hamburgers, fresh corn, chocolate cake, and fresh tomatoes the runners up. What GI's disliked most was raisin pie, followed by rice pudding, asparagus, liver, and—you guessed it—spinach.

U.S. aid helps Greece clear stricken land of Red guerrillas,

uts railway into shape and feeds suffering people.

1951 was the year when fear of war reached its highest peak. There were shopping scares in the great cities, and sales went up 25 per cent in the department stores, as people scrambled for canned goods, electric equipment, nylons, and the like. SHAPE, Eisenhower's headquarters near Paris, was formally activated in April, and an acrid debate split the country about sending GI's back to Europe. The Marshall Plan and ECA helped to strengthen and stabilize the democratic governments of Europe and thus checked further Communist advance in Western Europe. Truce talks began in Korea. Few people had any idea how many anxious, grinding months would pass before peace materialized.

Meantime, the United States discovered, almost overnight, that its frontiers were expanding with unprecedented speed and scope. Everybody

But prime beef was still scarce and crazily expensive all over the nation, way into 1951. Mike DiSalle, OPS boss, urges further price controls.

No country except U.S. could produce this picture, which shows amount of food the average American family eats in a year. Householder is Steve Czekalinski, flanked by wife and 2 children. He works in DuPont plant in Cleveland, earns $1.96 an hour, spends $1,300 a year on food. Among items are 698 quarts milk, 131 dozen eggs, 2 crates oranges, 56 pounds butter, 450 pounds flour, 350 pounds sugar, 180 loaves bread, 300 pounds beef, 39 pounds coffee, 8½ gallons ice cream, 690 pounds potatoes, 1 sack onions, 31 chickens, and 2 turkeys. It took 4 men 20 hours to assemble food in picture, and total weighed 2½ tons.

People begin to take nuclear air raid precautions seriously, although some people hide behind trees in what seems to be an amateurish manner. Revelations of awful, inconceivable power of new weapons frighten populace, but perhaps do not frighten it enough.

Age of the alert descends upon us. New York cop surveys Fifth Avenue, totally devoid of human traffic.

B-50, refueled by aerial tanker, is ready for instant retaliation in case of enemy attack.

knew that we were in Okinawa, and intended to stay there. But now we learned that five massive American air bases were going to be built in Morocco. Their construction would be the largest peacetime job ever handled by the army engineers. The purpose of these bases was, of course, to give a perch for our bombers in the event of sudden war with the Soviet Union. And we stretched fingers north as well as east and west. The United States signed an agreement with Denmark for the defense of Greenland, and a contingent of American troops arrived in, of all places, Iceland. On the other side of the world we negotiated a mutual defense treaty with Australia and New Zealand, extending American commitments into the Southwest Pacific, and work began on a similar pact for the Middle East. But we did not know that we would get nowhere with this until we understood better the new forces of Egyptian and Arab nationalism, and stopped treating new nations patronizingly like children just let out of school.

Fear of air raids increased. Cities learned laboriously how to hide their citizens, if the citizens were

willing to be hidden.

But what was happening to the American character, the American soul, during all of this? Almost all of us still believed devoutly in peace, but were we in danger of becoming militarized against our will through the sheer grisly pressure of events? We were still a free people, and proud of it, but could we withstand any further insidious assault on our cherished civil liberties?

133

Newspapers of the nation, during all this period, did their job under markedly increasing difficulties. Labor costs went up, and good editorial talent became scarcer. One phenomenon was a steady shrinkage in the total number of newspapers, and the growth of monopoly. Many important cities— Milwaukee, Atlanta, Des Moines, Kansas City, Omaha—were served by only one newspaper or, at best, by several newspapers under the same ownership. Luckily most of these were good newspapers. New York City, which boasted not many years ago of a dozen newspapers, was reduced to five, not counting tabloids. The ancient and honorable tradition of personal journalism seemed to be declining. Newspapers long noted for their dignity of make-up became crudely vulgarized, and, rather than take a strong editorial line themselves, newspaper proprietors hired columnists who, as often as not, bewildered readers who wanted to know what the paper stood for by canceling each other out on the same page.

But, in spite of various timidities, pressures, and evasions, our newspapers did at least remain free. And we got

all points of view.

Far away in Argentina, the Perón dictatorship closed down "La Prensa." That, at least, is something that could not happen in the United States.

However, to say that our newspapers are "free" does not mean necessarily that they are free enough. Robert M. Hutchins, for many years president of the University of Chicago and later head of the Fund for the Republic, an offshoot of the Ford Foundation, had this to say not long ago:

"The purpose of a newspaper, and the justification for the privilege of the press, is the enlightenment of the people about their current affairs. No other medium of communication can compete with the newspaper in the performance of this task. A newspaper that is doing this job well is a good newspaper, no matter how deficient it may be in astrology, menus, comics, cheesecake, crime, and Republican propaganda. . . . A newspaper that is doing this job will have to bring before its readers points of view with which it disagrees and facts that it deplores. Otherwise in monopoly towns the people cannot expect to be enlightened, for television and radio are unlikely to be in the same class with a well-run newspaper in telling what is happening and what it means. Television and radio are, moreover, controlled by a government agency, and one that does not inspire much confidence today."

Some observers worried too about what the pressure of strident and glib commercial advertising might be doing to us. Certainly the United States is, above all countries on earth, the one where advertising and publicity are noisy kings. Listen to George F. Kennan of the Institute of Advanced Study at Princeton, in a speech at Notre Dame: "The immense impact of commercial advertising and the mass media on our lives . . . tends to encourage passivity, to encourage acquiescence and uniformity, to place handicaps on individual contemplativeness and creativeness."

American journalism remained the most independent and vigorous in the world. Such newspapers as the "Times" and "Herald Tribune" in N.Y., the "Christian Science Monitor," the Washington "Post," and the St. Louis "Post Dispatch," among others, knew how to do their job, and did it.

William Randolph Hearst, who feared nothing but death, died in August, 1951, aged 88. Fantastic old man left behind him a legend, a fortune, and a complex dynastic situation.
He rides merry-go-round on last birthday at fabulous San Simeon ranch.

"New York Times" celebrated its hundredth birthday. Today one Sunday issue "uses more ink and paper than went into the entire first year of the Times." Its solid tradition, comprehensive news gatherings, and impeccable professional standards and integrity make it greatest of world's newspapers.

"Meet the Press," one of nation's most aggressive TV-panel shows, makes Martha Roundtree, its producer, a renowned figure in Washington politics and society. She greets Perle Mesta.

Russians officially subsidize sports as agency of national policy, make powerful bid for Olympic titles. Soviet "amateurs" are mostly pros.

Champion Bob Mathias won decathlon in 1952 Olympics, setting new world and Olympic record. But Russians almost won games.

Ted Williams, "rudest" man in baseball, says good-by to empty stands at Fenway Park, Boston, before rejoining Marines. Williams was highest paid man in big leagues, probably ranked as most valuable player of decade.

Sport, before **1951** at last gave way to **1952**, suffered several scandals. Crime, gambling, and racketeering ate their way into amateur athletics. Audiences with keen noses had, for some time, suspected that college basketball games were being "fixed." There are people in the United States who gamble on the number of flies that will settle on a screen door in a given period, or whether the next girl entering a bar will be blond or brunette. The nation's annual gambling bill was around twenty billion dollars. It was inevitable that gamblers should make a racket of betting on points made in games like basketball. Fourteen players or ex-players from colleges in New York City confessed to fixing games, and three stars from Bradley University, in Peoria, Illinois, were indicted by a grand jury in New York, together with eight gamblers. Long Island University canceled intercollegiate sports and City College (New York) canceled its basketball season, while the authorities *tried to clean up.*

At about the same time the US Military Academy at West Point dismissed 90 students—including most of the football team—for academic irregularities. What, people asked in horror, was happening to our youth? But this did not keep them from attending avidly the games that youth played. And in a variety of sports we had champions old and new to watch, like Bob Mathias, Ted Williams, and Rocky Marciano. Money spent at spectator sports beat all records in 1951—$3.8 billion.

Few baseball players have been more universally admired and popular than Joe DiMaggio, great hitting Yankee outfielder, now retired.

Jersey Joe Walcott, knocked out in 13th round after leading on points, loses world's heavyweight championship to hard-slugging Rocky Marciano.

$70,000,000 liner "United States," biggest and most luxurious ship ever built in U.S., broke all speed records on maiden voyage, crossed Atlantic in 3 days, 10 hours, 40 minutes.

Americans like heroes, as do most other people on the earth's surface. Also Americans tend to forget heroes quickly. Who remembers Captain Carlsen now? But anyway he and his "Flying Enterprise" gave us vicarious

pride and excitement

on a theme that is as elemental as any—the struggle of man against nature. And anyway Americans still have the inestimable and let us hope inalienable right to pick our heroes by popular democratic instinct, and not to have them shoved on us from above.

Meantime the US sent tourists to Europe by the hundred thousand. What, one might ask, did the average European think of in connotation to the term "American"? Skyscrapers, neon-lit filling stations, predatory gangsters, pretty legs on pretty girls, great roads that slice a continent like a cake, Hollywood, hamburgers, and men wearing shiny, ugly, brown walking shoes. And of course—notoriously—the US was "materialistic, devoid of aesthetic interest, naïve, politically confused, raw, inhuman, provincial, emotionally immature, and devoted exclusively to the art of making money."

Maybe.

Opening days of 1952 brought epic uplift to Americans, as news came of Captain Henrik Kurt Carlsen's heroic efforts to save freighter "Flying Enterprise." Carlsen, alone except for one man, refused to leave sinking, lopsided ship, fought to save it in raging gale, almost won.

New vistas enchant young Americans. Tourists jam their way onto planes and ships for crowded European holidays. Roads became almost impassable and prices rose steeply, but nothing can detract from gilded charm of towns like Venice.

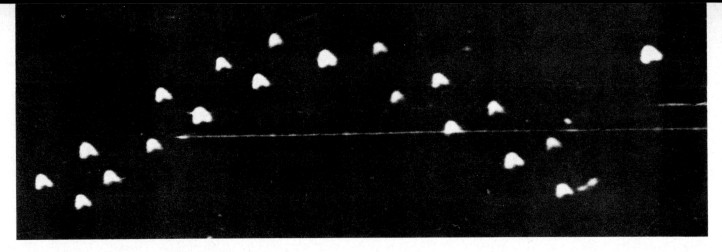

Visions of flying saucers make tantalizing controversy. Maybe the man in the moon is visiting us, but maybe not.

Alexander Calder makes "mobile"
sculptures out of wire, wood, aluminum,
paper, and other odd materials—
particularly wire—so that
objects attached move, and, in words
of one critic, resemble solar system.
Calder, in middle fifties, started playing with wire
at age of 8. Other exciting American artists of
decade were mostly abstractionists.

Another example of new dimensions
in vision effected by artists
and scientists—photographs
of lunar landscape taken by world's
most powerful telescope,
Mt. Palomar, Calif.

What were we talking about at home as the good year **1952** advanced? Well, for one thing, flying saucers. Reports from all over the nation came in from people who attested that they had seen these mysterious aerial "objects," and science fiction writers and others made a fine morbid hullabaloo with reports of dwarf men and other unnatural specimens visiting us from outer space. And sober aircraft pilots testified to witnessing and in some cases chasing celestial phenomena of a sort never encountered before. But no airplane ever caught up to one. One American pilot, however, crashed at 30,000 feet while pursuing a mysterious object in circumstances never fully explained. The Navy said that the saucers might be high-flying balloons. The Air Force began a long investigation and announced finally that the saucers were probably "natural phenomena"—mirages. But thousands of people remained convinced that the saucers were not only real, but represented sinister reconnoitering expeditions from another world.

All manner of other developments, some of them more frightening than the saucers, came in man's attempt to lift himself further off the earth, and propel engines

further into space.

A pilotless navy plane made a new world's record of 1,300 miles per hour at 70,000 feet, and a Viking rocket set another by going up 135 miles. Proposals came for the first atomic airplane, and it was announced that a B-36 so powered would, in theory, be able to fly around the world 80 times on one pound of U 235, the equivalent of something like six million gallons of gasoline. Work on atomic power plants for submarines advanced. New bomb tests rocked the bleak sands in Nevada, and atomic artillery became a fact,

Movie goers wear polaroid glasses to gape at new 3-dimensional films. Experiment didn't last long.

with consequences revolutionary to warfare on the ground. Radio-controlled pilotless planes, with television sets for eyes, were launched by aircraft carriers off Korea and bombed enemy targets. But all this was overshadowed by another event vastly more terrifying. Work on the hydrogen bomb progressed "satisfactorily," and in November the United States detonated for the first time a thermonuclear device near Eniwetok. This was probably the most destructive explosion ever made by man up to that date. Light from the blast "looked like ten suns." An entire island disappeared.

*   *   *

At home we had comelier things to watch, like Vivien Leigh, who won an Academy Award for her performance in "A Streetcar Named Desire," and a newcomer

both dulcet and sultry,

Marilyn Monroe. Movies we liked—our mood was still escapist—were "The Greatest Show on Earth" and "Singing in the Rain." Some good books were

Stunning performance by Gary Cooper (here with Katy Jurado) in "High Noon" made this clean-cut, understated picture the best Western in years. Few noticed that it also presented Grace Kelly in her first non-bit part.

Enter Marilyn Monroe. A graduate from "art" calendars, she symbolized a tough-sweet amalgam of prettiness and sex. Ambition: to be a good actress. Real name: Norma Jeane Mortenson.

published, like Rachel Carson's "The Sea Around Us," which opened our eyes to the fact that the world, as well as ourselves, consisted mostly of water. Alistair Cooke won a well-deserved TV award.

There came a frightening epidemic of airplane accidents, and Newark airport was closed after a crash in which former Undersecretary of War Robert Patterson was killed. **1952** took, incidentally, a painful toll in other useful lives. Jo Davidson died; so did Harold Ickes; so did Gertrude Lawrence, Philip Murray, Senator McMahon, and the venerable philosophers George Santayana and John Dewey.

Mr. Truman seized the steel industry to avert a nation-wide strike, but was overruled by the Supreme Court. The Senate killed statehood for Alaska by one vote. We discovered to our consternation that several Collectors of Internal Revenue, to whom we paid taxes, were crooked, which seemed to be adding insult to injury. And we were pleased—all of us not prejudiced—by steady ameliorations in the field of race relations. 1952 was the first year since 1882 without a lynching. The Supreme Court barred Jim Crow on railway cars, and wonder of wonders, the exclusive New England school Groton took in its first Negro boy.

Another stunning performer, José Ferrer, shortens his legs to give vivid, realistic impersonation of French painter Toulouse-Lautrec in "Moulin Rouge."

Charlie Chaplin, greatest and most enduring of all movie personalities except Greta Garbo, turns himself into a clown for "Limelight." Picture, though disappointing in part, showed Chaplin's sublime artistry. He became expatriate after picture was released.

Crime made its usual overburden of ugly news throughout the year, and there came a rash of attempted jailbreaks. What worried responsible citizens most was a steep and menacing growth in juvenile delinquency and teen-age hoodlumism. Youngsters—some of them under fifteen—

mugged, mauled, robbed,

and ran. Of 1,100,000 arrests in 232 cities, more than 147,000 were of boys and girls under 21, a shocking commentary on the moral health of the nation.

McCarthy during the year kept slam-banging at the State Department. But his tactics changed to an extent. His main targets were diplomats in the

Narcotics traffic continued to be one of country's ugliest phenomena. Here dope suspects attempt to repel photographer.

eenage gangs fight in Harlem. teep, ominous growth of juenile delinquency became a asty unsolved problem in U.S. ities. Youngsters almost as avage as "wolf-children" in ost-revolutionary Russia efaced American streets, errified communities, nd committed almost a uarter of nation's crimes.

Willie Sutton, notorious long-sought bankrobber, was arrested following tip to police by a Brooklyn youth, Arnold Schuster. Three weeks later Schuster was murderously shot down by unknown thugs. Crime scandalized New York.

field or officials in Washington who had influenced China policy—John Carter Vincent, John P. Davies, and John S. Service. The McCarthy technique was to insist that, with so much smoke, there must also have been fire, and to return to the attack again and again. The Lattimore case dragged on. And so did the Remington case. And there were other cases in which the crudest type of witch-hunting played a role. But also nests of defiant fellow travelers were exposed, and the term "Fifth Amendment" became fixed in the language in a manner not foreseen by the authors of the Constitution. Meantime most Communist leaders still at large were picked up by the FBI in a series of drastic roundups. This was essential to the national safety, and, under the Smith Act, perfectly legal. But it was still not a crime to be a Communist, unless you worked for the overthrow of the US Government by violent means. If, however, you were named by some bigot as a Communist "sympathizer" you could get into plenty of hot trouble.

Mickey Spillane's detective stories, compounded of gunfire, lust, and sadism, sold by the million, appealed to debased juvenile taste not only in U.S. but abroad.

1952 was, of course, a presidential year, and we dutifully gave way to the joys and excitements of a quadrennial national spectacle that is half massacre, half carnival. The 1952 campaign differed from any other in recent years in several striking respects. First, both conventions were wide open. For the first time since 1928, the incumbent in the White House was not a candidate. Second, never for more than half a century did the outs have to face a party that had had five full consecutive terms in office. Third, nobody was sure of new patterns in the electorate, with its vast pools of untried voting power. Fourth, this was the first election fought under the pitiless glass eye of television. Fifth, two prominent candidates, Harriman and Stevenson, had been divorced—three if you count MacArthur. This was not important, but it was a phenomenon quite new. Sixth, more intraparty bitterness was expressed than in any campaign since the McAdoo-Smith fight in 1924. Few people remember today the icy venom attending the Eisenhower-Taft struggle for the Republican nomination. Seventh, this was the first campaign since 1920 in which a military man was a candidate.

Politics becomes major U.S. preoccupation as 1952 campaign gets under way. Here are two well-known American couples, smiling with good reason.

Texas played central role in Chicago convention storm. Republican National Committee, controlled by Taft, claimed Texas delegation. But "fairplay rule" put over by Ike supporters helped swing votes to Eisenhower.

The chief advantage the Republicans had was desire of the people for a change. The Democrats had been in power for twenty uninterrupted years, and that is a long time in a democracy run under the two-party system. Give the Democrats another four years (said the Republicans) and the two-party system will be as dead as the show that closed last Saturday night.

The chief advantage the Democrats had—or thought they had—was that they, not the Republicans, were now the majority party in the country. The polls showed that, in an estimated electorate of 55 million, 21.5 million voters would be Democrats, 18.5 million Republicans, and 15 million independents. So the Republicans, to win, had to make enormous inroads on

the independent vote.

The principal issues were Korea, "the mess in Washington," McCarthy, high taxes, and foreign affairs. Extremists talked about "twenty years of treason." Truman was vociferously accused of being a "warmonger," at the same time that he was belabored for not pushing the Communist Chinese beyond the Yalu. The Taft Republicans, who wanted to cut aid to Europe, were on the other hand aggressively interventionist in regard to the Far East. They wanted, so it seemed, to risk giving way to Communism in Europe, while attacking it in Asia. They were defeatist on one front, belligerent on the other, although they must have known that the world was round.

Fittingly enough, Sherman Adams is in center of this picture. Virtually unknown outside New Hampshire when campaign opened, he quickly became one of Eisenhower's most intimate advisers, was "Acting President" during Ike's illness in 1955.

Eisenhower drank a light Scotch and soda after the nomination, and at once called on Taft, who was bitterly disappointed by defeat.

Estes Kefauver, capitalizing on his renown as a crime investigator, fought hard for the Democratic nomination, lost, and did not like losing.

Truman and Stevenson, men of totally dissimilar type united in a common cause, are heroes of frenzied convention.

Also, to make confusion worse confounded, Eisenhower, the Republican candidate, had been a major executant of the Democratic foreign policy!

Corruption did not turn out to be much of an issue. Americans like crime-busters, and this was one reason why Kefauver gained an early lead on the Democratic side. But, in the immortal if scandalous words of Will Rogers, "It's awful hard to get people interested in corruption unless they get some of it."

Ike announced that he was a Republican and would accept a "clear-cut call to political duty" early in January. He won thumping victories in the New Hampshire and other primaries while he was still in Europe. He returned to the United States, and made his first political speech at Abilene, Kansas, in June. He won the nomination, as everybody knows, with Richard Milhous Nixon (whose wife had once been a Democrat) as his running mate. Eisenhower's own words, delivered at a press conference much later, about the way Nixon happened to be chosen, are the following: "The first thing I knew about the President having any great or any Presidential nominee having any great influence in the Vice-Presidential nomination was, I think, about . .

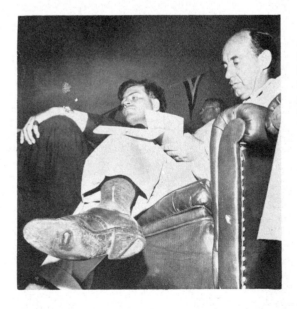

Adlai had shoes re-soled after this photo was published. Stevenson conducted campaign on high level, and added to contemporary politics an ingredient it sadly lacked—wit.

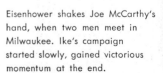

Eisenhower shakes Joe McCarthy's hand, when two men meet in Milwaukee. Ike's campaign started slowly, gained victorious momentum at the end.

148

the moment that I was nominated. And I wrote down—I said I would not do it—pick one man—I didn't know enough about the things that had been going on in the United States. I had been gone two years. And so I wrote down the names of five, or maybe it was six, men, younger men, that I admired, that seemed to me to have made a name for themselves. And I said, 'Any one of these will be acceptable to me,' and he [Mr. Nixon] was on the list."

Ike's campaign started slowly, and seemed inept to many. He wanted to be President, but found it painful to have to work like a politician for the presidency.

He did his best to heal

sore wounds within the party. He came together with Taft, and Stevenson promptly quipped, "Taft lost the nomination but won the nominee."

On the Democratic side, Truman announced in March that he would not be a candidate to succeed himself. So other candidates arose. Stevenson did not want to run. He wanted another four years as governor of Illinois,

Bingo craze advances. 1,000 desperately earnest players assemble in a New Jersey church hall after referendum made game legal.

Chlorophyll, which is what makes grass green, becomes big business as a deodorant. Hundreds of chlorophyll products sell in drugstores.

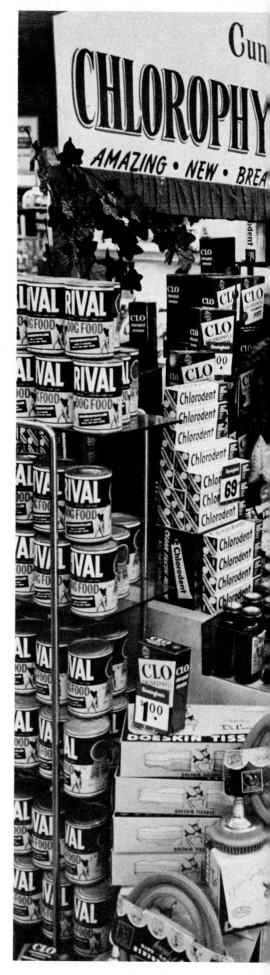

and then—perhaps—he might try for the presidency. The pressure of party leaders was too strong for him, and it can be said of this wise, spirited, and elevated man that he was one of the few Americans in history ever to be nominated for the presidency against his real desire. Senator John J. Sparkman of Alabama became the vice-presidential nominee.

The campaign that followed the conventions was extraordinarily lively, even for America. One sensation was the revelation that Mr. Nixon had accepted eighteen thousand dollars for political expenses from friends in California, a circumstance which he explained in a full-dress performance on TV. Another was a promise by Eisenhower that, if elected, he would go to Korea, see the front for himself, and work for an honorable peace. One thing continued to impress observers who could manage to stay above the furor of the battle, namely that this was a fight between two extraordinarily decent and attractive men. Moreover they were probably the two most modest candidates in presidential history. Ike said, "My brother Milton has the brains of the family." Adlai said, "I am temperamentally unfit to be President."

Mr. Eisenhower won triumphantly. We all know that.

It was hard, during all this agitated time, to keep our minds on the *minor excitements* and pleasantnesses of life, on games and fads and hobbies. But the chronicler should record dutifully that this was the year when chlorophyll became a huge business. Girls began to wear their hair like poodles. New York State banned the game of bingo, because it induced gambling, and yellow oleomargarine became legal almost everywhere. The country spent $254 million on chewing gum, and $26 million on playing cards. People began to say "Good-by now" instead of merely "Good-by," and the verb "dig" became a synonym for "notice" and "like." Pizzas competed with hamburgers, and more and more men wore nylon shirts and Dacron suits, in order to avoid wrinkles and save laundry bills.

150

"Budgies"—small parakeets—
became a rage. They were cheap,
pretty, and could talk, something
most other pets can't do.

Scrabble sends millions of people
flying to dictionaries or each other's
throats, even as crossword puzzles
did a generation ago.

Communist bomb explodes in Saigon, wrecking cars, killing ten. Viet Minh agitators begin new phase of Indo-China struggle, which ended by forcing French withdrawal from northern half of country.

UN, magnificent city within a city, seems untroubled while quietly dominating N.Y.'s East Side skyline.

Russia since the war has incorporated the following countries into the Communist orbit—East Germany, Poland, Estonia, Latvia, Lithuania, Rumania, Bulgaria, Hungary, Czechoslovakia, Albania, China, Manchuria, Inner Mongolia, Outer Mongolia, the northern half of Korea, and Tibet. A lot. And we Americans did not know at this time that, on its own home front, the Soviet Union was making gigantic strides in the development of long-range bombers and guided missiles, and would have the H-bomb soon—much sooner than American experts anticipated. Moreover its industrial capacity was being augmented steadily.

At this time, **1952,** it was the Far East that concerned us most. First Korea. Next Indo-China. That seemed to be the Soviet program. A complex struggle for power had proceeded in Indo-China since the end of the Japanese occupation, and this flared into open, ugly warfare. Ho Chi Minh, a powerful revolutionary and leader of the Viet-Minh nationalist movement, attempted to set up an independent republic. Behind him were not merely the Communist party and Chinese Communists across the border, but a great many Indo-Chinese patriots who were not Communists at all—men who hated the past, hated colonialism, and hated French rule and would do anything to get rid of it. It was impossible to keep nationalist sentiment down, and the Communists—to compress crudely developments of the greatest intricacy— hijacked the nationalist movement. The French, not the most adept of colonial rulers at best, paid the price for shortsightedness, refusal to appreciate the contours of the modern world, and plain selfishness. And soon the flower of the French Army was fighting in Indo-China—fighting a war, moreover, that was almost *certain to be lost.*

Much the same kind of unhappy development came in North Africa later.

Japan became a sovereign state again in April—World War II was now officially over—and it was a matter of urgency to see to it that Japan, remade in a manner of speaking by MacArthur, should continue to rest firmly in the American camp. As to Korea the truce negotiations, a year old, still went wearily on. A principal abrasive issue was that of repatriation of prisoners. The Communists sought to make headlines with the monstrous and totally mendacious charge that the United States had engaged in "germ warfare."

153

Ancient Japan starts new life, as U.S. occupation ends. Communists break up Socialist and trade-unionist meeting and demonstrate against Americans

And there were other troubling spots in Asia, the Middle East, and Africa, for prudent Americans to watch. That strange creature Mohammed Mossadegh, dictator of Iran, broke off relations with Great Britain, following trouble over oil. Civil war continued in Malaya. The Naguib-Nasser coup took place in Egypt, and the malodorous reign of King Farouk came to an end. The Mau Mau rebellion broke out in Kenya, and the Gold Coast and Nigeria came closer to independence.

As to affairs in Europe we saw West Germany, like Japan, become a sovereign state at last. American, British, French, and other troops took part together in elaborate NATO maneuvers, and six Western nations (France, West Germany, Italy, and the Benelux countries) joined up to create the European Defense Community, on French initiative. The Schuman Plan went

American Legion's 37th annual convention, isolationist zealots accuse UNESCO, a valuable UN agency, of spreading "subversive" educational material.

into effect, and western Europe began to pool its coal and steel resources. Maybe the valiant old dream of western European peace and unity was coming true. At any rate Washington hoped so. The best guaranty of peace was a virile, indissolubly united Atlantic Community, and if this really came into being the peace might not be lost—after all.

At times our European

allies became restive,

though. The United States was at this period practicing a policy of "containment," more or less, vis-à-vis the Soviet Union. Even so, some Europeans thought that America was becoming too trigger-happy for full comfort, and that some crazy people might want a preventive war.

And now we reach **1953.** The most important event early in the year was, obviously, the inauguration of President Eisenhower. Ike shocked the protocol-minded by refusing to wear a top hat—he wore a black Homburg instead—and was pleased that his son, Major John Eisenhower, was among those present. (It was Mr. Truman who had ordered him home for the occasion.) Eisenhower hoped for a simple, inexpensive inauguration, but it did not quite turn out that way. The five-hour-long parade included Indian chiefs, an

Bess Truman takes Mamie Eisenhower through White House before inauguration, pointing out what's what. They are not weeping, but have head colds.

Only two living ex-Presidents, Harry S. Truman and Herbert C. Hoover, watch Mr. Eisenhower become 34th President. They know, among other things, what he's in for.

Chief Justice Vinson administers inaugural oath to new President in Jan., 1953, as world watches. Eisenhower's address dealt mainly with foreign policy and peace.

Alaskan dog team, a Kansas stagecoach, and a monstrously impressive atomic cannon, the first ever to be publicly displayed.

Clearly this was going to be an administration led by businessmen. Charles E. Wilson of General Motors became Secretary of Defense and George M. Humphrey, an Ohio banker, took the Treasury portfolio. John Foster Dulles (Secretary of State), Herbert Brownell, Jr. (Attorney General) and James C. Hagerty (press secretary) were all "Dewey men." Henry Cabot Lodge, who had done as much as any man to win the nomination for Eisenhower, became head of the US mission to the UN, Harold E. Stassen took the post of Mutual Security Director, and Sherman Adams, former governor of New Hampshire, became an indispensable member of the official family. One surprise was the appointment of a Democrat, Martin P. Durkin, as Secretary of Labor, but he did not last long.

The country, which had wanted a change, and now had it, scrutinized these and other new faces. This was a new deck, if not a new deal. Almost everybody, politics quite aside, wished the new administration well.

Mr. Eisenhower promptly ended wage controls and price controls on con-

Ike named Charles E. Wilson of General Motors Defense Secretary. Wilson had to give up $2½ million worth of GM stock before taking post, shocked many by a misquoted remark seeming to compare General Motors to the country. Here Wilson laughs with Michigan Senator Homer Ferguson.

sumers' goods. Rent controls were, however, extended. The national budget showed a deficit of more than $9 billion, a peacetime record, and it became clear—to the outraged disappointment of some Republicans—that there would be *no tax cuts this year.*

The President took a step long needed, and established a new Cabinet portfolio for health, education, and national welfare, with Mrs. Oveta Culp Hobby of Texas as its first Secretary. He took the presidential yacht out of service, and sent his brother Milton on a good-will trip to South America. He appointed Charles H. Bohlen to be Ambassador to Moscow, and tasted for the first time inflamed opposition in the Senate, when the McCarthyites balked, but were defeated. (Bohlen had been at Yalta, and was hence damned.) He appointed Earl Warren to be Chief Justice of the Supreme Court, when Mr. Vinson died, set up plans for a meeting at Bermuda with Churchill and the Prime Minister of France, whoever that might be when the time came, and in a speech to the UN proposed that all nations, including the USSR, should pool part of their atomic stockpiles for peaceful purposes.

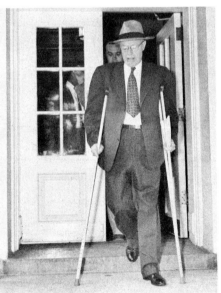

Robert A. Taft, mortally ill, leaves the White House after conference with politically inexperienced President. Taft, a virtual "prime minister," helped Eisenhower greatly in early days of administration, and his death was a severe loss.

Pretty Elizabeth, 55th monarch and 8th reigning queen in eleven centuries of British history, rides to Westminster Abbey in her glowing jewel of a state coach, with Duke of Edinburgh at her side, as Coronation festivities approach vibrant climax. Most of the world was made happy by this panoplied event, which symbolized unity of crown and people.

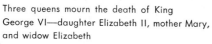
Three queens mourn the death of King George VI—daughter Elizabeth II, mother Mary, and widow Elizabeth

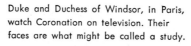
Duke and Duchess of Windsor, in Paris, watch Coronation on television. Their faces are what might be called a study.

King George VI died in February, 1952. Princess Elizabeth and her husband, the Duke of Edinburgh, happened to be on safari in Kenya, and on that night were perched high in a verdant fig tree at Camp Treetops, one of the most unusual hostelries in the world. Elizabeth went up the tree a princess, and *came down a queen.* Her coronation took place on June 2, **1953.** The British royal family is one of the most highly prized of American institutions, and Elizabeth—for the period of the Coronation anyway—was not merely queen of her own domains but of the United States as well. We loved the magnificent ritual of the Coronation ceremony, we loved the Queen's impeccably handsome husband, and above all we loved the Queen. But all this did not keep a fierce little war from breaking out between rival American broadcasting companies struggling to get the great event to television screens first.

This month also saw the conquest of Mount Everest, which made it a British month indeed.

159

Dwight D. Eisenhower, playing golf at Augusta, Georgia, greets a bowing admirer—his five-year-old grandson Dwight D. Eisenhower.

One of the strangest paradoxes in American public life is that, although the power of politicians depends on the people, most people don't like politicians. And the fact that Mr. Eisenhower was—manifestly—not a politician added substantially to his

prestige and popularity.

This was no dingy ward heeler feathering his nest in the name of "public" service; this was no gummy or brazen manipulator trying to buy votes for favors. He was honest, wholesome, and humane. But was he strong enough, fixed enough in his own ideas, commanding enough in leadership, to be a good President? Did he have enough intellectual power and stamina? Would he have guts enough, savvy enough, to put his program through?

His own hope was, it seemed, to be a kind of supra-party President, above politics. He wanted to drive straight down the middle of the road, as leader of all the people. But increasingly it became difficult to determine what was the "middle" of the road, if he did not define carefully where the curbstones were. A friendly, tactful man, he hated fights. He would have loved it—ideally—if he could have been nominated for the presidency by the Democrats as well as the Republicans. But soon he learned that no President of the United States, no matter how idealistic, can live in an ivory tower and be a head of state as European monarchs are. He was active leader of the government in power, which meant that under the American system he had to be the active party leader too.

Yet Eisenhower had no concrete political experience. He had never run for office, and had seldom even voted. He had a genius for conciliation and building up and running a good team. But, some of his critics felt, his military background led him to depute authority too much. He left too many important decisions to members of his staff.

We learned that Mr. Eisenhower liked to play golf, and stayed away from the White House more than was common. We learned that he did not care for paper work, and disliked much of the routine of the presidency. But he believed in good human and social relationships, in the unity of the country, and in peace. He was a military man, but nobody could have been more earnest, more devoted and sincere, in his quest for peace.

He said once, "I hate war as only a soldier who lived it can, only as one who has seen its brutality, its futility, its stupidity." On another occasion (before he became President), he told a graduating class of civilians, "Your business is to put me out of business."

Many backwater Republicans thought that he was too liberal. He ardently believed in free enterprise, but it became clear that most of the social gains of the New Deal would be maintained. There might be whittling down of such institutions as TVA and Eisenhower may have viewed with private antipathy the principle of the welfare state, but no wholesale attempt to turn the clock back occurred. In his first State of the Union message Mr. Eisenhower asked for wide expansion of social security, continuing support to agriculture, and a health reinsurance program. Before long he was asking for a "soil bank" for farmers, an experimental flood insurance program, federal aid to education, and a relaxation of the country's immigration laws.

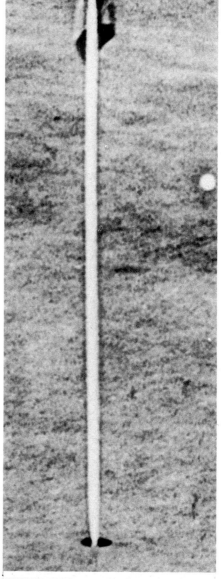

Spectacular shot by Lew Worsham won $25,000 purse in Chicago tournament. At 18th hole, Worsham needed a 2 to win, 3 to tie. He got the 2 by a miraculous 110-yard final shot, which dropped into hole that he could not even see.

29-1 outsider Dark Star beats favorite Native Dancer in 1953 Kentucky Derby.

His regime was conservative, but it was not going to be reactionary. As one eminent historian put it, "The liberal conception won, in a sense, its greatest triumph in the election of 1952 when the Republican party, as the party of conservatism, accepted as permanent the changes wrought in the American scene by a generation of liberal reform."

In 1953, it is important to remember, Eisenhower was not the figure of positive myth that he became later. He was still on trial. He was an honorable and friendly man digging his way into the problems of the presidency, not yet a legend.

* * *

Sports occupied us too. Two new cities entered the major league circuit, when the Boston Braves moved to Milwaukee and the St. Louis Browns to Baltimore. The Supreme Court confirmed an old ruling that baseball was a sport, not a business, even though players could be bartered or sold by owners like sheep. The Yanks monotonously won their fifth consecutive World Series, and football had a lively year. Florence Chadwick set a record by swimming the English Channel in 14 hours 42 minutes. For the fourth year in a row Australia beat the United States to hold the Davis Cup. This grieved us, because Americans, who can be infantile on occasion, proverbially like to be ***the best in everything.***

66,280 fans see Alabama squash Syracuse, 61-6, in Florida's Orange Bowl. 66,281st spectator was in airplane 1,000 ft. up taking this picture.

Yankee Mickey Mantle (No. 7) hits 4th grand-slam homer in World Series history.

Science fiction, almost as mechanized as science itself, remains a febrile reading craze—

Arthur Godfrey fires Julius La Rosa, demands "humility" from flock. Newspapers blow up scandal to something roughly equivalent to end of world.

The nation had 186 TV stations by **1953**, and 27,600,000 sets. New Jersey began broadcasting educational films as part of its school system, and a medical school in Colorado telecast the birth of a baby for the first time over a national hookup. Controversy over color TV proceeded litigiously, and in black and white we enjoyed programs like "What's My Line?" and "Kukla, Fran, and Ollie." TV had become, if possible, even more of

a demoniac craze

than in previous years. Many people thought that TV was cheapening and vulgarizing the nation, by inflicting on millions of helpless viewers the lowest common denominator in entertainment, but on the other hand it became clear that, if properly developed, it could greatly augment the

is translated into TV programs like "Captain Video," featuring bizarre, metallic adventures.

Christine Jorgensen, ex-G.I., was a transvestite (someone with "morbid desire to dress in clothing of opposite sex") and went to Copenhagen, where Danish physicians transformed him into a "woman" by surgical procedure. Comely Miss Jorgensen has had interesting career as an entertainer ever since.

national sophistication. In the remotest hamlet in the country, people could see, if they wanted to, just what Adenauer and Mendès-France looked like or how Japan conducted an election—to say nothing of events in the realm of art and science. One shrewd observer reported after a trip through the most culturally desolate wastes of the Middle West, "TV means that Main Street has disappeared."

But, during this period, other personalities concerned us aside from TV stars like Edward R. Murrow, Bishop Sheen, and Imogene Coca. Death came to Robert A. Taft, and Senator Knowland of California took his place as Republican floor leader. Trygve Lie retired as Secretary General of the UN, because of Soviet pressure, and was succeeded by another Scandinavian, Dag Hammarskjold. Irreverent newspaper headlines called him just "Dag,"

Pianist Wladziu Valentino Liberace tickles women's fancy as well as keys. Here he makes up eyes.

165

Proud papa Desi Arnaz of TV's immensely popular "I Love Lucy" took this portrait of his family.

Ford Motor Company spent $500,000 to celebrate its 50th anniversary with an elaborate two-hour show, precursor to today's "spectaculars."

since "Hammarskjold" was too long a name to be convenient. General Marshall won the Nobel peace prize, and other Nobel prizes went to Winston Churchill (now Sir Winston) and Dr. Albert Schweitzer. Mr. Eisenhower made James B. Conant High Commissioner to Germany, and Dr. Nathan Pusey succeeded him as president of Harvard. Young Robert F. Wagner became mayor of New York City, as the Democrats won five out of six off-year election fights. Comment from Eisenhower: "I have lost skirmishes before."

And much else happened on the national scene. Prices continued to rise relentlessly. Coffee was now 90 cents a pound, and the New York City subway fare went up to 15 cents. General Motors voluntarily boosted wages, even though its contract with labor still had two years to run, and steelworkers won an 8½¢ an hour raise from the US Steel Corporation without a strike. The AF of L and the CIO took tentative steps toward a merger, and promised not to raid each other for members. Atomic bomb tests continued resonantly in Nevada. Girls began to wear "Italian" haircuts. The Bricker Amendment, which embodied the last gasps of the old isolationists and aimed to hamstring the President's constitutional treaty-making power, annoyed the administration. Eisenhower was, it seemed, having more trouble from his own Republican right wing than from the Democrats. The President asked Congress to let 240,000 displaced persons into the country, and Senator Wayne Morse

Old faces give way to new. Radio Crooner Rudy Vallee greets TV crooner Eddie Fisher.

High spot was joint appearance of Ethel Merman and Mary Martin, an event greeted by fans as something little short of celestial.

TV's "Miss Frances," Chicago educator, makes small children happy with Ding-Dong School.

of Oregon, a stubborn independent, made the longest speech in Senate history—22 hours 26 minutes—in a vain attempt to save tideland oil for the federal government. At 11:02, Eastern Standard Time, August 10, the population of the US became exactly 160,000,000. To save money, the Department of Defense ordered a 10 per cent cutback in army and navy manpower. Here again a familiar American paradox was repeated. We wanted to have a positive foreign policy and be strong, but hated to spend the money.

*   *   *

Meantime we watched delectable creatures like Miss Audrey Hepburn, and relished **the vivid competition** among Hollywood producers to make movies in three dimensions. "Tea and Sympathy" opened on Broadway, and so did "Teahouse of the August Moon." Seldom has homosexuality, which was a growing concern in some circles, been treated with such candor as in the former play, discriminatingly acted by two people named Kerr, Deborah and John.

We looked at such performances avidly. We also watched, but with consternation, the uproar caused by the case of Harry Dexter White. Attorney General Brownell charged in a speech that White, who died in

1948, had not only been a Soviet spy when he was Assistant Secretary of the Treasury, but that the FBI had reported his activities to the White House, which nevertheless—far from firing him—promoted him to a better job! The nation spluttered. The House Committee on Un-American Activities sought to subpoena Mr. Truman, but Truman would not accept the subpoena and talked to the country on TV instead. J. Edgar Hoover politely contradicted Truman's explanation to the effect that White had been kept on so that the FBI could the more easily keep on watching him. And then Mr. Eisenhower said that it was "inconceivable" that Mr. Truman could have appointed a

CinemaScope made movies look "like a slot in the mailbox," said one early critic, but audiences voraciously welcomed it.

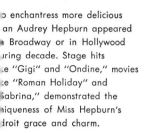

o enchantress more delicious an Audrey Hepburn appeared Broadway or in Hollywood uring decade. Stage hits e "Gigi" and "Ondine," movies e "Roman Holiday" and abrina," demonstrated the niqueness of Miss Hepburn's droit grace and charm.

Communist spy to high office knowingly, and that somebody else at the White House must have been at fault. It was all very confusing, to say the least.

No fewer than three different Congressional committees were now at work hunting out Communists and making furor. One was the old House Un-American Activities Committee, the chairman of which was Harold H. Velde of Illinois. In the Senate we had William E. Jenner (Indiana) heading an Internal Security subcommittee of the Judiciary Committee, and Mc-Carthy was chairman of the Permanent Investigations subcommittee of the Committee on Government Operations, of which he was also chairman. By reason of the Republican victory these chairmanships had all gone to Republicans, including McCarthy, and this was an important development. McCarthy sent two of his young men, Cohn and Schine, roaming through Europe to check on the purity of books in United States Information Service libraries. A great deal of miscellaneous smearing went on. Even an actress like Lucille Ball was not spared.

But *something of a change*

in the national mood began. What might be called a revolt of the decent started. The worm turned. Mr. Velde got into a peck of trouble by suggesting that the Protestant clergy in the US was Communist-infected. President Eisenhower in a speech at Dartmouth denounced "thought-control" and book-burning. As a result of the activities of Cohn and Schine in Europe, a few books, idiotically enough, had actually been burned. Most important,

Meantime Cinerama remained a solid, exciting hit. Cinerama screen consists of hundreds of strips of plastic tape, and gives a 3-dimensional illusion.

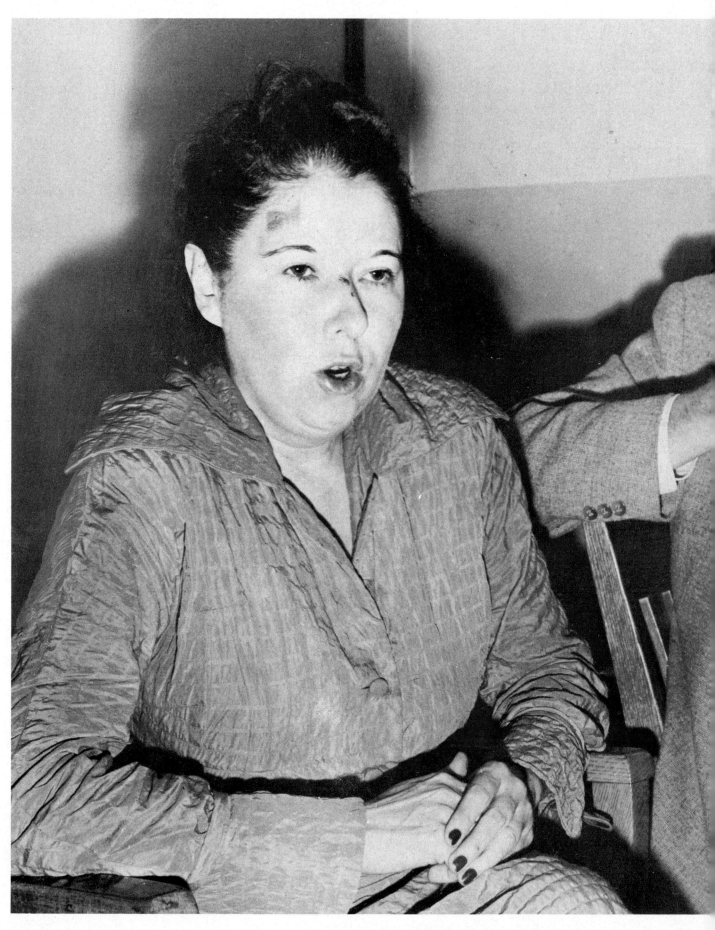

Two of most vicious murderers in U.S. annals were dope addict Carl Austin Hall and Bonnie Brown Heady, prostitute and alcoholic. They kidnapped 6-year-old Bobby Greenlease in Kansas City, Mo., shot him, and got $600,000 ransom. Police had them behind bars within a week.

McCarthy seemed to have overreached himself. He was forced to drop J. B. Matthews as his chief investigator, as a result of uproar over the church issue. The three Democratic members of his subcommittee took a walk. Also he got into trouble with Dulles and Stassen by intruding into their provinces. And it was clear by this time, even if Mr. Eisenhower did not say so, that Mr. Eisenhower took a low view of most of his activities. Then McCarthy announced that he was going to investigate an "extremely dangerous" Communist spy ring in the Army, no less, at Fort Monmouth, New Jersey. And the Army was not pleased.

We took time out—some of us—to try to take stock. Were we still a free people? What were we so afraid of? What point was there to being the richest nation on earth, if all the money went to armaments and taxes? What were we doing for peace? And what good would it do us to win the Cold War, if it cost us democracy at home?

*   *   *

Sociologists do not find it easy to explain why the United States is more addicted to crime than any civilized nation. There is no simple reason. A number of factors come into play—the superabundant physical vitality of the United States, its mixedupness, desire for quick moneymaking, contempt for law, our migratory effervescence, the tradition of ruthless direct action inherited from frontier days, and the

irresistible urge

of people to advance rapidly from class to class. The emigrant from, let us say, Puerto Rico, hears about crooked politics, and sees no reason why he should not be crooked too. The bright kid in the filling station out West wants to buy a fur coat for his best girl, and robs the till.

At any rate the American crime sheet, during these years, stood at an appalling figure. A major crime was committed somewhere in the United States every fifteen seconds. What a country! There were on the average 20 murders a day, 600 automobile thefts, and 3,300 larcenies. New York City had an average of 311 major crimes a day, including 3 rapes, 27 felonious assaults, 31 robberies, and 140 burglaries. And a worrying factor everywhere was a steep rise in the use of narcotics.

Houston, Texas, jailers use TV cameras to keep watch on prisoners, which "improves" conduct. System calls to mind George Orwell's novel, "1984."

William Faulkner,
4th U.S. author to win the
Nobel prize in more than half
a century, created the most
profound image of Deep
South extant in American
letters, with his skilled, pas-
sionate portrayal of Yokna-
patawpha County. Faulkner is
often mocked for obscurities
and unending, almost unintel-
ligible marathon sentences,
but he has fierce artistry
and has written some of the
most moving—as well as
some of the most throbbingly
morbid—stories in the English
language.

No new titans emerged in the American world of letters in this decade. There was no new novelist of the stature of Sinclair Lewis, no new critic as provocative and astringent as H. L. Mencken, no new poet who sang with the aromatic bittersweetness of Edna St. Vincent Millay. Promising newcomers emerged in several fields, yes. But they did not give the giant taste of Wolfe or O'Neill or, among the living, Sandburg and Frost. We read admirable carefully carved short stories by John Cheever, Jean Stafford, J. D. Salinger, Truman Capote, Eudora Welty, and many others. But by and large our best writers were the veterans—Steinbeck, Faulkner, Hemingway. And they were very, very good.

As to **1953**, best sellers were "Désirée," by Annemarie Selinko, which proved that people still liked costume romances, Catherine Marshall's "A Man Called Peter," which proved that they liked religious inspiration, and "Sexual Behavior of the Human Female," by the celebrated Dr. Kinsey, which proved something else again. As to magazines, "The New Yorker" survived the death of Harold Ross and maintained its expert and enlightened standards. E. B. White and Charles Addams were still with us.

One trend in books was a vast improvement in the nature of titles in cheap, soft-cover reprints. Another was the forceful swing from

fiction to nonfiction.

For years slick serials were the main attraction in women's magazines, but now the emphasis was on articles. The convulsions of real life made fiction seem pale. It was hard to be interested in John's love for Mary when the atom bomb was sizzling right around the corner. Besides, as a European philoso-pher once said, the greatest of American superstitions is belief in facts.

Ernest Hemingway likes to write about the soul of man under pressure. His theme is almost always the conquest of love by death. Hemingway became a legend before he was 30—for his life as well as works—and has had a stronger, more piercing influ-ence on present-day world literature than any American writer. A magnificent artist, he has never written a line of junk in his life. He miracu-lously escaped two airplane crashes in Africa in 1954, and won a long-deserved Nobel prize for his lyrical "Old Man and the Sea."

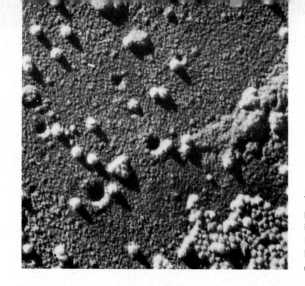

Scientists devise apparatus which smokes 60 cigarettes at once, for research into possible relationship between nicotine and lung cancer. Meantime millions of Americans turned from conventional to filter cigarettes.

This is first authenticated picture of isolated poliomyelitis virus, greatly magnified. Incessant research on polio led subsequently to development of the Salk vaccine.

Mental illness, we learned to our discomfiture, was now the number-one health problem in the United States. More than 700,000 people were in mental hospitals, and more were pouring in day by day. What, we might well have asked, was driving us so crazy?

In particular schizophrenia was on the increase, and so were types of mental ill-health afflicting young people—adolescents and GI's home from the wars. Hospitals devoted to mental cases were at least 30 per cent overcrowded, which meant that nobody got "optimum" treatment, and roughly 40 per cent of all beds occupied by mental patients were in obsolete, deteriorated, or even condemned buildings. And, of course, the hospitals were grossly understaffed. There were institutions (and these were among the best) where forty psychiatrists had to take care of sixty-five hundred patients.

One significant and in fact sensational shaft of hope came in 1953 with the development of the new "miracle" drugs, reserpin and chlorpromazine. These seemed to promise astonishing ameliorations in several types of mental illness, and already have accounted for a 19 per cent speed-up in the dis-

Reserpin, drug derived from anciently known Indian snake-root, has extraordinary effects in alleviating certain types of mental illness. So has chlorpromazine, a synthetic compound first made in France.

Tuberculosis death rate has been cut 75% in a decade, largely by the use of new antibiotics like streptomycin. Trudeau, a famous old sanitarium in Adirondacks, closed down when its few remaining patients moved to state hospitals.

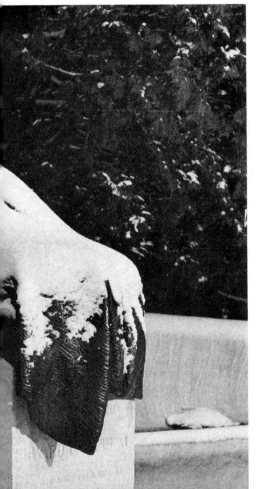

charge rate in some state hospitals. But a great deal more needs to be done, particularly in research. The federal government in 1953 allotted $18,000,000 for basic research in all fields of medicine—not just mental illness—which was exactly .00029 per cent of the national budget and considerably less than what went to the study of plant and animal diseases. Yet we are supposed to be a rational country. From private sources came about $40,000,000 for medical research. Perhaps this may seem to be a tidy sum. But in the same year the country spent $5.3 billion dollars on tobacco and $1.5 billion dollars on jewelry and watches.

One profoundly important and beneficent development this year had to do with infantile paralysis. Scientists at the University of California isolated for the first time the virus that causes poliomyelitis, and Dr. Jonas E. Salk of Pittsburgh and his associates announced that their experimental vaccine (made out of monkey kidneys) would be ready for widespread use next year. Millions of parents waited,

breathless with hope.

Stalin died on March 5, **1953**, at the age of 73. He had been dictator of Russia for twenty-nine uninterrupted years, and few men have ever written their names on the pages of history with more brutal, sinister, and cryptic force. We did not know at this time that the Russians would soon repudiate his memory. His first successor as Prime Minister was his protégé Georgi M. Malenkov, who made a triumvirate with Molotov and Lavrenti P. Beria, chief of the secret police. But Beria's days were counted. A police state, in the end, almost always devours its own children, if its children do not devour it. Malenkov and Molotov ganged up on Beria, and he was calmly, neatly executed for "criminal activities." At this time few people outside the Soviet Union knew much about Nikolai Bulganin, who was to succeed Malenkov as Prime Minister before long. And another dignitary little known, Nikita S. Khrushchev, shot up and became Secretary General of the Communist party, and thus the most important man in Russia.

Obviously the new Russian regime needed time to consolidate itself, and a tentative *"peace offensive"* got under

UNITED STATES   UNITED KINGDOM   UNION OF SOVIET SOCIALIS

Clare Boothe Luce, former play-
wright, actress, and Congresswoman,
presents her credentials
as American Ambassador to Italy.
Italians, unused to women
as diplomats, did not realize at
first that Mrs. Luce was both
cleverer and more serious
than most men.

Death comes to Josef
Vissarionovich Djugashvili,
hated, feared,
and obeyed by millions.
Soviet Union's iron-minded,
implacable dictator-deity
was 73.

way. Malenkov said that there were "no controversial issues that could not
be settled peaceably." But we learned in August that the Russians had successfully exploded a hydrogen "device," and President Eisenhower announced
that the Soviet Union was now in a position to make an atomic attack on the
United States. Big news.

In his first speech as Secretary of State Mr. Dulles took what critics thought
was a somewhat tactless line, when he warned western Europe that it "must"
achieve unity. Congress, getting into a mood of boredom with international
affairs, a phenomenon not infrequent, passed a bill to cut off all foreign aid
by June 30, 1956, and all military aid a year later. Presumably our legislators
thought that, to save a dollar or two, we should be prepared to stand off the
hostile world without allies. What a confident country the United States has
always been! Meantime, however, the administration held fast to its basic
prudent line. After abrasive negotiations, we obtained the right to build air
bases in Spain. And we carried the Cold War to a new front by sending

Lodge laughs, Jebb scrawls,
Vishinsky ponders, at meeting
of UN Security Council.
Vishinsky asked not
to be called a "gentleman,"
and Lodge thinks it's funny.

Bold German youngsters hurl
stones at Red tanks, and
attempt vain revolt against
East Berlin regime. Disturb-
ances were quickly sup-
pressed, but they showed
that the spirit of resistance
behind Iron Curtain is not
yet dead.

177

A few American prisoners in Korea refused repatriation, decided to stick with Communists. Families in U.S. sent them transcribed appeals to return.

food to East Germany. Plans for the European Defense Community suffered disconcerting setbacks. The French, exhausted by the war in Indo-China and paralyzed by strikes at home, refused to accept any arrangement whereby West Germany would be rearmed. Negotiations for a four-power conference of foreign ministers dragged on wearily, with the Russians becoming more obdurate. Yugoslavia and Italy

continued to quarrel

over the nut of Trieste, as the US and Britain withdrew their occupation troops. Mr. Dulles, addressing a NATO conference, passed from warnings to veiled threats, spanked the French, and said, "If the Western European nations are going to commit suicide they may have to commit it alone."

By far the most vital, agonizing issue in Europe was German unification. We had to do our utmost to support West Germany, in order to avert the long range possibility that it would be drawn into the Soviet orbit. So—the irony does not need to be labored—West Germany became not merely our ally but the linchpin of our European policy. And West Germany began to prosper mightily (as did Italy) while France and Britain suffered. A man from Mars might well have asked who won the darned war, anyway.

On the Asian front corollary developments took place. Early in the year

Some American P.W.'s were forced by captors to carry banners praising Communist regime.

V. K. Krishna Menon, left-wing Indian delegate to UN, reports to Prime Minister Nehru. Menon tried to bring both sides together in Korean talks.

Eisenhower "unleashed" Chiang Kai-shek, that is, withdrew the Truman order by which the Seventh Fleet stood by to prevent any action by the Chinese Nationalists on Formosa against the China mainland. We donated substantial help to the French in Indo-China, sent arms to Siam, and gave Pakistan wheat. A new and tough little country, Burma (the only state except Eire ever to withdraw from the British Commonwealth), refused to accept any further United States aid, on the ground that we were supporting Chinese Nationalist guerillas on Burmese territory. In the Middle East the quarrel between Israel and the Arab states endangered peace. Further away, the Sudan (almost four times the size of Texas) reached the threshold of independence. The British realized that they would soon have to leave Suez. Still further away, the nationalist government of Dr. Daniel Malan, which has been described as the ugliest government in the free world, further entrenched itself in power in South Africa.

Truly the whole world had become our frontier. Everything was interlocked. There was no phase or field in international relations that we could afford not to watch.

Finally—at long last—peace came in this year to torn Korea. Almost until the last moment there were serious American casualties. There had not been much ground fighting in 1952, but in 1953 the North Koreans and Chinese

179

Cease-fire in Korea comes at last, August, 1953. UN soldier looks warily at Chinese and North Koreans across No Man's Land.

Communist officer examines one of 22,000 Chinese and North Korean POW's who wanted to stay on our side, and were freed.

Syngman Rhee, President of South Korea, tough and tenacious despite his 78 years, bitterly opposed Korean truce, saying it would mean death to his nation.

made savage attacks. General Van Fleet said angrily that we had the Communists completely on the run back in 1951, but were "tricked" into

prolonged truce talks.

A Senate subcommittee found that American lives had been "needlessly lost" because of serious ammunition shortages. Meantime, until the armistice was signed on July 27 (**1953**), damaging combat continued in the air as well as on land. In all the United States Air Force destroyed 823 MIG's, with many others probably destroyed or damaged. We on our side, using many old bombers and support ships, lost no fewer than 971 planes, but only 58 were Sabrejets. One curiosity was the offer by General Mark Clark of $100,000 and political asylum to any Communist pilot who flew a MIG-15 across the lines and delivered it to us intact. The offer was made in April, and five months later, sure enough, a North Korean boy defected, brought a plane in, and got the reward, although he said he had never heard of the offer.

This was the first war ever fought by the United States that we did not win with the possible exception of the War of 1812. Some people said that if Truman and Acheson had made the Korean peace, and not a Republican administration, they would have been impeached. But the great majority of Americans, the overwhelming mass of citizens, were overjoyed that the war was over. The boys were coming home. And, some years later, Mr. Truman summed it all up with the words, "We could not stand idly by and allow the Communist imperialists to assume that they were free to go into Korea as elsewhere. This challenge had to be met—and it was met. It had to be met without plunging the world into general war. This was done." But the cost was grievous. Total American casualties were 137,051, including more than 25,000 dead in battle.

The chief issue during the paralyzingly tedious armistice negotiations was that of prisoners. We had roughly 100,000 prisoners; the Communists had roughly 16,000, of whom 4,451 were Americans. Many of the prisoners we held were conscripts or others who detested the Communist regime, and who

South Korean woman, devout follower of Rhee, weeps as she kisses South Korean flag, symbolically placed on ground, as demonstration against terms of truce.

Pro-American Ramon Magsaysay becomes President of Philippines. He is happy and so is U. S. Magsaysay, a vivid character, fought the Huk guerrillas.

181

Sons come home, after three grinding years at Korean front or in enemy camps.

wanted at all costs not to be repatriated to Communist territory. And we felt that we had no moral right to turn these unfortunates back to the tender mercies of their Communist masters. Eventually voluntary repatriation was agreed upon, with India heading a five-nation commission for the custodianship of POW's, and screening teams were set up to interview each man. The exchange of prisoners who wished to be repatriated was known as "Operation Big Switch," and was concluded on September 6. The UN turned back to the Communists 75,799 prisoners, and the Communists turned back to us 12,760. About 22,000 Communists chose to remain on our side, and—alas—

a handful of our men,

including 23 Americans, chose to remain with the Communists.

During all this we had troubles with our ally, the venerable and gristly Mr. Rhee. He fought stubbornly against the truce terms, and, on one dramatic occasion, illegally set free thousands of anti-Communist prisoners in flat defiance of the UN.

We did not know it at the time, but these negotiations brought us to the "brink" of general war. Mr. Dulles disclosed later, in a celebrated magazine article, that the United States had warned Communist China, through the person of Prime Minister Nehru of India, in June, 1953, of our intention to bomb Manchurian bases with atomic weapons if the Communists did not sign the Panmunjom armistice.

Seven-year-old California girl greets her father, who spent 34 months as a prisoner.

Troopship from Korea arrives in Seattle. G.I. off boat continues to kiss his sweetheart after rest of crowd departs.

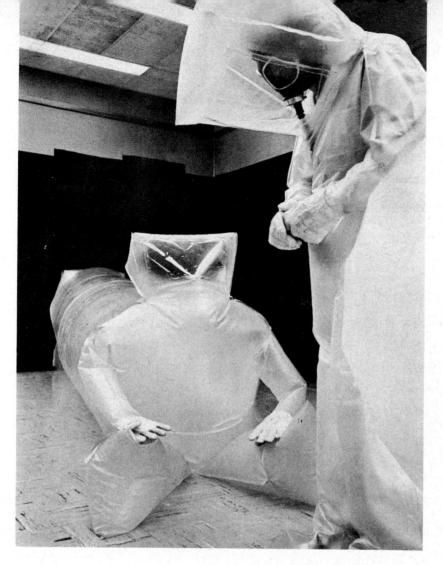

Atomic plant workers crawl through tunnel into plastic "suits" entering contaminated areas.

This is what desolate Colorado Plateau looks like.

And now came **1954.** We have reached yesterday. Probably the most blazing event of the year was the double comeuppance delivered by the US Army and Senate to Mr. McCarthy. But other occurrences came in other fields. Five Congressmen were wounded when a gang of Puerto Ricans started shooting at the floor from a spectators' gallery, causing a wild melee. The longest dock strike in the history of New York (29 days) tied up the waterfront, and cost about five hundred million dollars, which is not tiddly-winks even for the US. Scandals were uncovered in the Federal Housing Administration, and it became known that the late Harold Hoffman, governor of New Jersey in 1935-38, wrote a letter before his death confessing that he had embezzled $300,000. We groaned. Were all politicians crooked?

Out West the hunt for uranium made a kind of contemporary Gold Rush, and prospectors like Vernon Pick became celebrated—and very rich. Chief source for the free world's uranium had been, since the war, the Belgian Congo. There, in a remote mine hidden deep in the African wilderness, was

the *indispensable material*

for all our atomic development. The bombs that won the war could not have been made except for uranium from the Congo. But the Congo was far away.

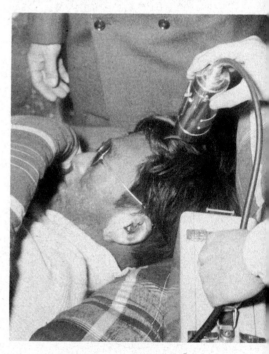

New word "fall-out" enters English language. In March 1954, U.S. set off tremendous thermonuclear explosion near Bikini. Japanese fishing boat, 71 miles away, was well outside what was considered to be danger area. But 23 crew members were burned or came down with radiation sickness, caused by fall of atomic ash.

Vernon Pick, lone amateur prospector, found fabulous uranium deposits here, after exhausting struggle. America still has a frontier.

And, conceivably, its treasures could be cut off in the event of World War III. Now South Africa was leaping into substantial uranium production as well as the Congo. Even so, the United States felt that it would be comfortable to have major sources of this metal closer to home. So the Atomic Energy Commission encouraged prospecting, and what has been called "the greatest minerals hunt of all time" started. Colorado was the favorite hunting ground, but many other areas were involved—northeast Washington, Nevada, and parts of Canada and Texas. (Texas, as usual, has everything.) Tens of thousands of prospectors, professional and amateur, went out into the hills. Geiger and scintillation counters became a big business, and were as much a part of the prospector's kit as a frying pan. And uranium ventures made weird, wacky news in the stock market. But, although traces of uranium are common over large territories, actual strikes are comparatively rare. Still, any ranchman on whose property uranium was found could become rich overnight, and a high school kid prospecting for fun on weekends might (so the dream went) find himself a millionaire. Almost all the conventional American attributes enter into this story—frontier spirit, Boy Scoutism, love of the big gamble, love of open spaces, enterprise, perseverance, competition for competition's sake, book knowledge translated into action, and the desire to get rich quick.

Pick was farm boy, owned Minnesota mill, believed in "self-sustenance homestead." Hs is certainly self-sustaining now, since he sold uranium mine he discovered near "Four Corners" (where Colorado, Utah, Arizona, and New Mexico meet) to Atlas Corporation for $9,370,000.

185

AEC and Civil Defense Administration co-operate to see what atom blast will do to an average house. Bomb was light and three quarters of mile away, but house burned in 2⅓ seconds.

Gigantic steel "eye," built near Schenectady, N.Y., for Atomic Energy Commission, will house atomic power plant for submarines. Ceaselessly American scientists explore edges of the unknown.

In March, **1954,** the United States set off a new series of bomb explosions in the Marshall Islands. Nuclear tests were, perhaps, becoming monotonous to our jaded taste, but nobody could ignore these

apocalyptic monsters.

The destructive power of the new weapon went far beyond what the scientists had calculated, and the fallout area was immeasurably greater. "The sun was obliterated." Appropriately enough—since the world now quite obviously had the power to burn itself up overnight—this was followed by an air-raid drill on a national scale, the most comprehensive ever held. Theoretically the United States had thirteen million fatal "casualties," with 2,175,000 people "killed" in New York alone. Meantime we learned that, near Denver, the Army was manufacturing a new "nerve" gas which was capable of "wiping out whole cities." The gas was colorless and odorless, and one sniff was supposed to be fatal in four minutes.

In September, 1954, Russian nuclear explosions also occurred, and these, coupled with the drastic revelation of what our own H-bombs could do, caused a major significant change in American foreign policy. Mr. Dulles had been talking about instant "massive retaliation" in the event of any attack, but, patently, this might not be wise or practicable if the USSR was now also capable of instant, massive retaliation. American policy since the war had, as we know, been based on the immense and formidable "deterrent power" automatically given us by our monopoly on nuclear weapons. But this monopoly was broken now, and the Russians had their own positive "deter-

Moving day in Los Angeles. But almost every day is moving day. Since 1940, L.A.'s population has increased by 146,000 a year, and city is now 3rd largest in U.S.

U.S. highways groan under stupendous burden. Without cloverleaf intersections traffic would be even more hopelessly, maddeningly snarled than it is.

rent power." So it behooved us to look about with caution. The wisdom and statesmanship of Sir Winston Churchill played a considerable role in effecting this transvaluation of values. Our allies, even more than heretofore, wanted to avoid incidents or provocation. So, gradually, and with many vicissitudes, we veered toward the idea of "coexistence"—competitive coexistence. It took some time before this concept bore any fruit, and there was always the possibility that it might have to be thrown out of the window, but anyway a new phase in relations between the US and the USSR began.

On the home front the atom continued to make big—and fruitful—news. More and more nuclear material was released to industry for peaceful use. Huge reactors were built to provide energy. Work began on the first civilian nuclear power plant, in which a few pounds of uranium will do the former work of millions of tons of coal. More than 130,000 people were engaged throughout the nation on atomic work, outside the government, and at least 350 companies were actively engaged in atom business. The AEC, which controlled all sources of atomic energy, fertilized private enterprise in all sorts of fields. Atomic gadgets, if that is the proper word, began to be tested in food preservation, fertilizer research, insect control, ore processing, construction engineering, photography, plastics, rubber, cigarettes, glass, toothpaste, and much else. Precious isotopes continued to give indispensable aid to medical research. Internationally the United States pushed hard for an "atomic pool," to which all nations producing atomic energy should contribute, so that nuclear materials would be available to all countries for peaceful use. But the Soviet Union refused to co-operate without a prior agreement for prohibiting atomic weapons.

*   *   *

Now, since this is a book about America, we have to mention the automobile once more. There were by this time fifty-six million cars on the roads, one for every three persons in the country, and demand was still voracious although,

if you knew your way

around, you could usually manage to get a cut price from a dealer on most models. And the nation had its millionth death in an automobile accident.

Some cities have luxury of elevated freeway system, like San Francisco. Here snakelike traffic lanes lead to Bay Bridge.

Porfirio Rubirosa, ex-son-in-law of Dominican Republic's perpetual dictator Trujillo, marries tobacco heiress Doris Duke, who could afford him.

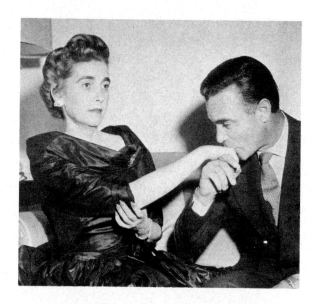

Next Rubirosa (who had once been husband of actress Danielle Darrieux) takes on Barbara Hutton, or vice versa. Marriage did not last long.

At same time playboy Rubirosa was playfully involved with Zsa Zsa Gabor, and presently Hutton wed German tennis star Von Cramm. World yawned.

Meantime —we became accustomed to such phenomena as the steady proliferation in motels, and the development of drive-in movies (which gave badly needed succor to the movie business), drive-in banks, drive-in shops, and even drive-in churches. The automobile kept shaking the country up like concrete in a mixer. Population patterns changed. California, a state created by migrations anyway, greeted more migrations. And patterns continued to change in automobiles themselves. Some people found it irksome to park or house cars that seemed to be as big as dinosaurs, and a certain vogue began for smaller, more agile foreign automobiles. Things that looked like metal bugs or worms appeared impertinently on streets and parkways. And, among American cars, the two-tone horrors began to carry all before them. You were not fashionable in some suburban circles unless you rode around in something painted chartreuse and mauve.

Americans, no matter how big most things are, want them bigger. And colossal mergers took place in the automobile companies. Nash married Hudson, and Studebaker married Packard. And this led to the possibility that the US might institute anti-trust proceedings against some of the major manufacturers. At this time three companies accounted for the production of 85 per cent of all cars in the country.

* * *

Not only was the country shaken up; families were shaken up. There were more than 390,000 divorces in the United States in **1954,** as against 1,546,000 marriages. The statisticians told us dolefully that

one out of every 3.8

American marriages ended in divorce, and a Gallup poll said that, if they had the chance to marry again, only 45 per cent of American husbands and wives would choose the same spouse. Children did their best to survive the wreckage caused by split families. There were boys in fashionable boarding schools in the East who, at the age of 17 or so, already had four or six or even eight different stepparents. No wonder many youngsters seemed (to their elders) unsettled and distraught.

Still, plenty of people managed to hang on to their husbands and wives,

Divorce courts and courts of domestic relations were tragically busy.

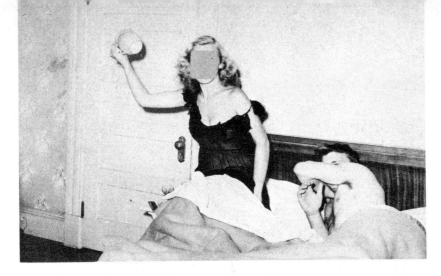

Divorce evidence is sought in hotel bedroom by Photographer-Detective Graham Moulton.

and some even had a good time doing so. Not all of us were Rubirosas, even if we would like to be.

And what were some other social modes and patterns? Americans drank a monumental amount of liquor, but not quite as much as is generally assumed. One poll showed that, of an adult population estimated at 102 million, roughly 60,000,000 people used alcoholic beverages, whereas more than 40,000,000 did not. But there seemed to be a sharp increase in drinking among very young people, with resultant bad manners and other unpleasant consequences. Another menace to the young was the huge popularity of "comic" horror books. And more and more grownups seemed to be taking astounding amounts of barbiturates and other relaxing drugs. Was reality so dreadful? Why was everybody so insecure?

The fabric of American life has so many strands, so many threads of different colors, that generalizations are difficult. Much of our seeming unsettlement was superficial. The neuroticism was only on the surface. One healthy trend was toward what might be called ease in living. People, particularly men, wore more comfortable, informal clothes. At the corner delicatessen you could buy almost any kind of food in precooked form, from esoteric imported soups to whole American-style dinners. Patterns in entertainment changed, and Café Society became enlarged by "Expense Account Society." Hardly anybody, millionaires excepted, could afford to go to chic restaurants any more, unless somebody else was footing the bill. And the very face of cities changed. Park Avenue—to cite one street in New York—became an avenue of glass, and a few blocks away the Third Avenue El was sentenced to disappear.

America murders a lot of people and a lot of people go to insane asylums and few countries are so given to eccentricities in social behavior, but, in spite of everything, most citizens remained sound. Many of those in institutions were merely aged. Headlines in the newspapers cried out with lurid sensation after sensation, but millions of honest folk never saw a mugging, never met a call girl, never got mixed up in a racket. A great many people managed to live quiet, normal, and eminently respectable lives, the major preoccupations of which were catching the 7:52 and worrying about little Johnny's cold in the head or did the house need a paint job this year.

Moulton has periscopes with cameras attached and other equipment. Here he watches outside door.

Toscanini had a symbolic importance far beyond his genius. What he symbolized—with all the controlled fire and tremendous dedicated intensity of his nature—was of course good music. Like the commander of an army, he converted the NBC Orchestra into a single soaring instrument, and brought it by radio into millions of homes, which became duly elevated. Another interesting and

effective penetration

of the American home with classical music came soon with the "Music Appreciation" records of the Book-of-the-Month Club, a worthy enterprise.

The first color TV set went on sale this year, but the image was small and the machine cost around $1,000. As to black and white TV, figures showed

Arturo Toscanini, one of sublime human beings of this or any time, passed his 87th birthday, and came near to breaking down while conducting farewell concert.

Classical music self-played is a rising hobby. Thousands of American music lovers form quartets, play mellow chamber music for their own enjoyment at home.

that the average TV-owning citizen now spent five hours a day in winter glued to the screen, three hours forty minutes in the summer. Viewers wanted more originality in programs, but did not find it easily. Arthur Godfrey buzzed the control tower cf an airport, and was grounded—if anybody cared. One popular song was "I Saw Mama Kissing Santa Claus."

"South Pacific" closed after a five-year run, and 3,500,000 people saw it, of whom it is safe to say that 3,499,999 liked the seeing. "The Caine Mutiny Court-Martial" opened, and so did "The Pajama Game." "The Seven Year Itch" was still running, and we had the perennial delight of seeing Alfred Lunt and Lynn Fontanne once more—this time in "Quadrille," by Noel Coward. "Porgy and Bess" (although we did not know it then) was soon destined to go to Moscow. "Abie's Irish Rose" was, incredibly enough, re-

vived, and, more incredibly, lasted for exactly 20 performances. Times do change. One interesting phenomenon was the popularity of small off-Broadway theaters, and the upsurge of new talent they encouraged. We trekked to the nether end of Manhattan and saw "Coriolanus" (not by a new talent, incidentally), "The Girl on the Via Flaminia," and "The Golden Apple."

Among movies, Cinerama wound up its second year as a triumphant hit, and "The Robe," a sumptuous mishmash of history and religion presented by CinemaScope, did terrifically well, although some people viewing it almost died of boredom. "Gone with the Wind," revived after 17 years, made nearly as much money as any new film. People—most movie makers to the contrary notwithstanding—do like quality, even if it was almost four hours long.

Alfred Hitchcock produced two nice little suspense movies during the year, "Rear Window" and "Dial M for Murder," and each gained signally by the presence of a new heroine who, it seemed, might be going places, the roseate Miss Kelly. Out in Las Vegas, the most notable of contemporary American Babylons, another heroine—Marlene Dietrich—proved the indestructibility of

her sirenish charm,

and earned thirty thousand dollars per week to boot. Miss Dietrich's appearance in Nevada typified a new vogue. Hotels and nightclubs paid fantastic amounts for eminent entertainers, because the gambling nearby could be counted upon to pay the bills. In Florida, too, although here gambling was not part of the picture, hotels equipped themselves for the winter orgy by trying to out Broadway Broadway, and the results were—even for Florida—spectacular.

As to books, Professor Toynbee gave us the last four volumes of his "Study of History," and "But We Were Born Free," by the veteran commentator Elmer Davis, did well and showed that a lot of Americans, in spite of everything, still felt keenly about civil liberties. Carl Sandburg compressed

Those who do not think George Gobel is a good comedian are a minority. Twenty-five million Gobel addicts listen to him faithfully every week.

Marilyn Monroe became Mrs. Joe DiMaggio briefly appeared in "Seven-Year Itch," joined Lee Strasberg's Actors Studio, organized her own film corporation.

The stout, extroverted, and hilarious Mr. Gleason never rests, recently signed a contract whereby he makes more money than anybody in history of show business. Gleason was virtually unknown five years ago. He is often funny.

Marlon Brando and Eva Marie Saint do well in an honest, brutal movie about a brutal subject—labor warfare on New York's racket-ridden waterfront. Story was by Budd Schulberg, music by Leonard Bernstein, direction by Elia Kazan.

his magnificent "Lincoln" into one volume, and "A Stillness at Appomattox," by Bruce Catton, won a Pulitzer prize. One verity exists above all others in the book business—that interest in the Civil War never falters. Much of the fiction published during the year was feeble, although many authors would contend that works of strength were ignored. The Library of Congress got its ten millionth book, and no doubt a lot of these books were feeble too.

Among commentators most of those who had informed the nation wisely early in the decade and before were off the air—Raymond Swing, William L. Shirer, Dorothy Thompson, et al. The valiant H. V. Kaltenborn still had a wide audience, which he well deserved, and so did Ed Murrow. There were few new giants. As to columnists the Alsop brothers were pertinacious, and nobody could match Walter Lippmann for insight, breadth of vision, and devotion to the public service. Anne O'Hare McCormick of the "New York Times" died, and this was a tragic loss indeed. James Reston helped ably to fill the gap she left.

53-year-old Boston lawyer Joseph N. Welch gained almost mythical renown by his handling of army side of McCarthy "trial." Welch's sly humor and puckish, Dickensian quality, plus sound legal brains and quick wit, made him a hero to millions.

McCarthy, grimacing, listens to youthful Roy Cohn, his chief counsel. Many did not like Mr. Cohn, but there were few who did not concede his ability. Whole case was broken open by Cohn's attempts to get favors for Private G. David Schine, his close friend.

And now came the most trenchant drama of the decade. Senator McCarthy took on the Army, or vice versa. Nobody who lived through this can have forgotten it, or

the emotional climate

it fed on. The United States faced an implacable enemy—the same enemy—both inside and outside our frontiers. Perhaps there had come some slight amelioration in domestic hysteria and perhaps on the international level we were approaching some kind of easement with the Soviet Union, but we were acutely nervous still—worried. On this atmosphere McCarthy continued to fasten, and the hearings of his committee (to which the Democratic members had now returned) became a phantasmagoria.

Outside the committee we were assaulted by corollary events. A man as irreproachable as Dr. Ralph Bunche was accused of "disloyalty," and had to go through the unhappy process of being cleared. There were backward areas in the country where, if you were overheard saying that you did not like Chiang Kai-shek, fanatics might report you to the FBI as a "traitor." Texas passed a law making membership in the Communist party a crime punishable by jail terms up to 20 years. A national magazine conducted a poll asking citizens how they identified people as "Communists," and got answers like "He was always talking about world peace," "She distributed literature about the United Nations," or "I saw a map of Russia on a wall in his home." Meantime acutely unpleasant occurrences abroad added fire to

Ray Jenkins, counsel for Senate Committee, was blunt in manner, strident of voice. Here he talks with a thorn in the McCarthy flesh, Senator Symington.

Famous—or infamous—cropped photo. To left is original shot of group including Army Sec'y Stevens and Schine; above is first version released by McCarthyites, to make viewers think that Stevens and Schine were talking chummily alone. It seemed that same man who doctored this photo could have fabricated the attempt to show Tydings and Browder together.

Edward R. Murrow, most distinguished commentator of decade, performed notable public service by objective, hard-hitting TV show letting McCarthy record speak for itself. McCarthy replied with half-hour filmed program rehashing old charges, and attempting to vilify Murrow. Until Murrow, most news commentators had tended to avoid coming to grips with McCarthy. Murrow's radio and TV work on such programs as "See It Now" and "Person to Person" won him innumerable awards.

One of stoutest Republicans in land, Ralph Flanders of Vermont, led Senate revolt against McCarthy. This prompted hearings by Senate Committee headed by a Republican equally conservative and rock-ribbed, Arthur V. Watkins (above) of Utah. Senate did its best to regain dignity it had lost in shambles of early hearings. McCarthy was not formally censured in so many words, but majority of Senate (67 to 22) dealt him a blow from which he has not recovered. He may—some day.

our fear and hate. We heard about American prisoners of war being tortured and "brainwashed." Thirteen Americans in China were sentenced to jail as "spies."

Such washing of spotted linen in public as that provided by the McCarthy hearings has seldom, if ever, been known in the history of a civilized nation before. Also the hearings provided bizarre and spectacular drama. Also they proved, if the matter needed proof, that the McCarthy technique made a travesty of Congressional investigations, although it was not disputed that Communists in high places should be rooted out. Also they left a bad taste in the mouth. Many people, listening to this

unprecedented display

of arrogance, brutality, and plain simple nastiness, left their TV sets feeling physically unclean.

But what unimaginably vivid theater it all made! Perhaps we hated it, but we could not tear ourselves away. Who will ever forget Mr. Welch's disclosure of the cropped photograph, or the carbon "copy" of the letter from J. Edgar Hoover, or the way Roy Cohn whispered intimately into McCarthy's cupped, wary ear? Who will ever forget the unfortunate Mr. Schine's first testimony, or McCarthy's impromptu reply to Senator Flanders, or the revelation that the Army monitored telephone calls between McCarthy and Secretary Stevens, or McCarthy's appeal to federal employees to go over the heads of their superiors and give him confidential data, or the time that Mr. Welch gave it as his opinion that a pixie was first cousin to a fairy?

Origin of the case was the McCarthy investigation of alleged subversion In the army laboratories at Fort Monmouth, New Jersey, and elsewhere. An army dentist, Major Irving Peress, appeared before the McCarthy committee and refused to answer questions about his Communist connections. At about the same time Peress got an honorable discharge. Sitting as a one-man subcommittee in New York, McCarthy savagely went after General Ralph W. Zwicker, former Monmouth commandant. When Zwicker refused to name officers involved in the promotion and discharge of Peress, McCarthy told him—a perfectly honorable officer with a gallant combat record—that he was not fit to wear a uniform.

McCarthy was riding high. Secretary of the Army Robert T. Stevens, who had only very limited experience with this kind of business, and who did not seem to understand fully the mannerisms of "Indian fighters" who kicked below the belt, defied McCarthy at first, then kowtowed to him humiliatingly, and in the end struck back. And so the immortal, incredible figures of Cohn and Schine re-entered the scene. One of the things the Army "had" on McCarthy, or thought it had, was the charge that McCarthy and Cohn, his youthful and undeniably brilliant chief of staff, had persistently asked special favors for Cohn's close friend G. David Schine, who had been drafted into the Army after trying very, very hard to get a commission. So the case came to "court"—before McCarthy's own Permanent Investigations Subcommittee of the Senate. McCarthy, however, stepped down as chairman, after Mr. Eisenhower made some pointed remarks at a press conference about the impropriety of a man sitting in judgment on his own case.

Anybody who takes on the U.S. Army is looking for big trouble.

The hearings lasted from April 22 to June 17, and produced a record more than 7,000 pages long. The verdict was mixed.

But this was not the end. The Senate got tired of being kicked around, and rose against McCarthy. The tide turned. There came another "trial," following charges brought by Senators Flanders, Fulbright, and Morse, which was conducted with propriety and due regard for the Senate's dignity, under the chairmanship of Arthur V. Watkins of Utah. The proceedings were not televised. A select committee of three Republicans and three Democrats voted unanimously to censure McCarthy for "conduct unbecoming a Senator" on two counts, after two weeks of hearings (August 31–September 13). Later the Senate as a whole watered the verdict down, and McCarthy was not formally "censured" but merely "condemned." But anyway this was enough to finish him—at least for the time being.

A footnote to this strange chronicle is that Congress, late in August, finally got around to outlawing the Communist party, largely as a result of pressure from Democrats. But membership in the party—let the lawyers figure it out—was still not a crime.

Willie Mays, great Negro outfielder, helps Giants beat Cleveland in 4 straight games in 1954 World Series. He saved first game by fantastic catch.

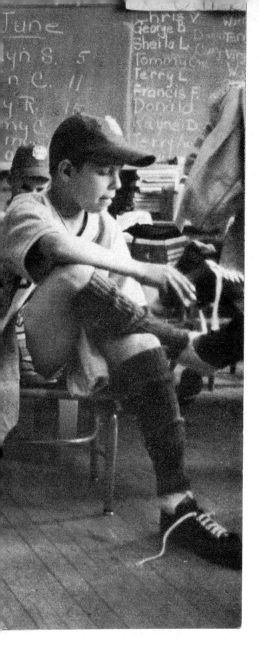

All over America "little leagues" proliferated. Kids 6 years old and above formed their own organized baseball teams, played through to a miniature world series. Diamond is one-third standard size.

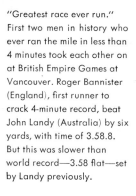

"Greatest race ever run." First two men in history who ever ran the mile in less than 4 minutes took each other on at British Empire Games at Vancouver. Roger Bannister (England), first runner to crack 4-minute record, beat John Landy (Australia) by six yards, with time of 3.58.8. But this was slower than world record—3.58 flat—set by Landy previously.

Another Giant hero was James Lamar ("Dusty") Rhodes, pinch-hitter who won first game with homer, helped score crucial runs in second and third.

Americans are apt to be somewhat chauvinistic about our prowess in sports, but it would be idle to pretend that we are the best in everything. No American ever ran a mile with the speed of Bannister or Landy. The Russians gave us a hard run in the 1952 Olympics, with even stiffer competition presaged for 1956.

In America, sport was not an agency of the state, athletes were not robots, and we still found

pleasure in sport

for sport's sake, even if some were commercialized. Victor Seixas became national tennis champion, and we won the Davis Cup back from Australia. Ed Furgol won the National Open golf title, and the courageous Babe Didrikson Zaharias won the Women's Open. A wonderful horse named Native Dancer retired, and an equally wonderful horse, Nashua, began to be heard about. The Giants beat Cleveland four games straight in a heady World Series, and the nation cheered, among others, Negro Willie Mays and his southern white teammate Dusty Rhodes.

Attorney Thurgood Marshall (center), shrewd and pertinacious, wins Supreme Court case, is congratulated by fellows. Counsel for Southern states was no less a personage than John W. Davis.

A great and germinal event came on March 17, **1954,** when the Supreme Court in a unanimous decision declared that racial segregation in public schools was unconstitutional. The new Chief Justice, Earl Warren of California, reading the decision, said that the old doctrine of "separate but equal facilities" should not apply to the field of public education, because separate facilities were inherently unequal. The ruling, which came after hearings contested on the highest level, was based on the Fourteenth Amendment. This was by far the most striking victory won by Negroes in their slow, stubborn fight

for equality of rights

and civil status during the decade—in fact century. Liberals everywhere rejoiced, if only for the fact that the United States, which stood for democracy all over the world if it stood for anything at all, was no longer vulnerable to the charge often leveled by Europeans that, in the matter of education for Negroes, it did not pursue democratic practices at home. But the South rose in agitation and alarm. The decision applied to 21 states and the District of Columbia; the states most affronted were, of course, those in the Deep South like Alabama, Mississippi, and South Carolina. Governors like Byrnes (South Carolina) said that the ruling was a serious blow to state's rights, but urged the people to preserve order. Governors like Talmadge (Georgia) said that "there would be no mixed schools in Georgia . . . and that the people would fight [sic] for their right to manage their own affairs."

New Negro stars Dorothy Dandridge and Harry Belafonte make blazing success of movie version of "Carmen Jones." Picture had all-Negro cast, entranced white audiences.

203

At once most of the South worked on means to frustrate the decision or delay its application. And, although we did not know at this time that a girl named Autherine Lucy would become the central figure of a vivid cause célèbre at the University of Alabama two years later, we learned quickly enough that passions over this matter, both in North and South, would not die out lightly. As southern intransigence became more inflamed, two schools of thought developed among responsible northerners. One was that the law must be applied with full vigor, even in the face of active southern resistance. The other advocated gradualism. Otherwise there might be something akin to civil war. Meantime some people, viewing southern reactions, called to mind a maxim from Booker T. Washington: "The white man cannot keep the Negro in the ditch without sitting down there with him."

And all during **1954,** a particularly crowded year, came a rush of other developments major and minor. The National Security Council grew to be

Carmine De Sapio, Tammany boss, confers with Averell Harriman, elected governor of N.Y. by thin margin in 1954. De Sapio would like Harriman to be President.

Adlai Stevenson, titular Democratic leader, greets Edmund S. Muskie, Democrat who won surprise victory to become governor of traditionally Republican Maine.

more important than the Cabinet, but the good old Cabinet struck out for modern ways by having one of its sessions televised for the first time. Charles A. Lindbergh, who had resigned his colonel's commission under FDR, became a brigadier general in the Air Force, and helped choose the site for the new Air Force Academy. Herbert Hoover, Jr., was named Undersecretary of State. Quentin Reynolds won $175,000 in a libel suit against Westbrook Pegler. The American Cancer Society reported that "heavy" cigarette smokers over the age of 55 have a 75 per cent higher death rate than nonsmokers.

This was a mid-term election year, and we wondered what the elections would say. How was Ike doing? What would be the verdict of the country about its first Republican administration in twenty years, when it hit the half-way mark? There was no doubt that Mr. Eisenhower, as a human being, was extravagantly popular, but some people felt that he lacked grip. The administration wanted to please as many citizens as possible, over the broadest possible arc, and sometimes floundered. Cabinet ministers got into the habit of contradicting each other (not a new phenomenon), and some, like Mr. Wilson, did not always seem to know what was going on in their own departments. Eisenhower carefully refrained from mentioning McCarthy by name in press conferences, not wanting to dignify him and hoping to avoid an irremediable spit in the Republican party, but this led to the charge that he was short on leadership. He did, however, like Truman, refuse to turn over

Another Democratic victor, Abraham Ribicoff, beat Governor John Lodge for governorship of Conn. by 2,800 votes. Ribicoff is escorted by state guard to inaugural.

secret security files to McCarthy.

American humor often has a note of the sadistic, and cruel little stories were heard—such as that a sign should be put on the White House saying "Eisenhower slept here once." After one press conference, when Mr. Eisenhower "broke every rule in the book" by his disarming candor and not only reversed the State Department on an important matter but also himself, an observer in the "New York Times" felt impelled to write, "Who but President Eisenhower could do these things and get away with it?" Yet Ike's political acumen and skill not only in press conferences but otherwise became more apparent day by day.

Eisenhower asked for an increase in social security to cover ten million more people, and cut federal price supports on commodities like cheese and butter, thus making these commodities cheaper to the consumer. He asked for a fifty-billion-dollar highway program, and was disappointed when Congress drastically cut down his proposals for low-cost housing and killed his health reinsurance plan. At the same time he pleased the business community by trimming the budget, substantially reducing taxes, and, in general, giving the strongest possible support to free enterprise.

Came the elections. The campaign was exciting. More people voted than in any off-year election in history, and results all over the nation were pinpoint close. The upshot was that the Democrats won control of both House and Senate. Their margin in the Senate was only one vote, and this was made possible by events in one state—Oregon. A bright Democratic newcomer, Richard Neuberger, won a close victory over the Republican incumbent there. In the House Sam Rayburn replaced Joe Martin as Speaker again. Also the Democrats won 18 out of 33 gubernatorial races. In New York, Averell Harriman beat Senator Irving Ives by the splinter of a hair.

In the last weeks of the campaign Mr. Eisenhower, against his inclination, was prevailed upon to make a quick campaign tour through several critical states, and said that there would be "chaos" and a political "Cold War" if the Democrats won control of Congress. Then, after the Democratic victory, he was quick to withdraw these rash words, and promised that he would not throw up any "roadblocks" in the way of "co-operation." Also he said, after one political address, "By golly, sometimes you sure get tired of all this clackety clack."

One result of the election was, of course, that the Democrats organized Congress and replaced Republicans in all committee chairmanships. McCarthy lost his chairmanships, retreated into shadow, and leaves this story.

America is, indeed,

an astonishing country.

Nothing is more difficult to predict than our political and other patterns. Normally one would have assumed that the Democratic triumph would, of necessity, be greeted as a repudiation of the Eisenhower administration. But not at all. The future was to show that the President got along better on the whole with a Democratic Congress than with his own. And consider the stock market. On the day after election, it went up, not down. In fact it had the biggest gain ever known on a single day since September 5, 1939.

After ferocious and dramatically publicized proxy fight, Robert Young of Chesapeake & Ohio won control of New York Central. Young, ex-Texan, was the man who first made it possible for a citizen to cross U.S. by rail without changing cars. He has been described as one of "ablest, brainiest, and most ruthless financial strategists in U.S."

Louis E. Wolfson, ambitious and fiercely energetic young promoter, attempts and fails to take over Montgomery Ward from octogenarian Sewell Avery. Wolfson, son of a Russian immigrant, now heads $231 million worth of enterprises.

Early in **1954** we had a minor slump or recession—maybe it was not so minor to those badly "recessed"—and unemployment reached 3,725,000. Mr. Eisenhower announced that "every legitimate means" would be used to avert a depression, and that "we must not and need not tolerate a 'boom-and-bust America.' " Business conditions improved by the end of the year, and soon the country presented once more an unexampled panorama of wealth, productive capacity, and purchasing power. The 1954 Christmas season was the most extravagant in living memory. The country during the year—to cite one figure—spent the staggering, unbelievable total of $68 billion on food alone. The total national income reached an all-time high.

One pregnant development, which we have neglected in these pages so far, was increasingly rapid industrialization in the South. New factories making plastics, chemicals, textiles, invaded moribund or placid areas below the Mason and Dixon's line. The South, which is the "problem child of the nation" not merely because of the Negro problem but because of its poverty, underwent a veritable industrial revolution. And there seemed to be at least a fair chance that, as it got richer, racial pressures would become less harassing and acute.

Prosperity on a nation-wide basis is, of course, a relative term. The country beamed and burst with wealth—but statistics showed that one out of every five new business ventures would die within a decade. We rolled (most of us) with plenty, but 75 per cent of all people in the country over the age of 65 had incomes of less than $1,000 per year. Geriatrics and care of the aged was, incidentally, becoming more of a problem than ever before, because, as a result of progress in medicine and other factors, more people

Edgar Dixon, president of $500,000,000 Middle South Utilities, Inc., and Eugene Yates, chairman of Southern Utilities ($780 million), gave their names to furiously controversial Dixon-Yates contract. Idea was to build immense new power plant for delivery of power to TVA, which needs it for AEC installations. Many businessmen in states involved as well as Democratic legislators fought Dixon-Yates bitterly, partly on ground that it was an attempt to stifle TVA. Administration backed plan at first, then cooled. Upshot—Dixon-Yates was abandoned.

tended to live longer. The nation had four times more men and women over 65 in proportion to total population than in the generation before.

And there were, of course, soft spots in the national economy that might well become softer. One was agriculture. We piled up an agricultural surplus worth more than seven billion dollars, and it was difficult, if not impossible, to get rid of this without wrecking farm prices at home or causing grave trouble abroad. Moreover, agricultural prices continued to go down sharply. Another possible soft spot was

an immense expansion

of consumer credit, i.e., people were borrowing too much money, in order to buy everything from automobiles to cream cheese. Another was, in the jargon of the experts, "a decline in the housing market," i.e., not so many people were building homes. The national debt was rising, and many reasonable people thought that the stock market was far too high.

Even so, the fact remained that we had probably reached a higher level of material well-being than any country in history. Sober economists said that, with luck, the very existence of poverty might be abolished in the United States within half a century.

General Motors produced its fifty millionth vehicle, and its president, Harlow H. Curtice, announced something unprecedented—a billion-dollar expansion program. Ford passed the billion mark in assets for the seventh year in a row, and—something else unprecedented—sold its stock to an eagerly waiting public.

One aspect of big business was, in addition to its vitality and confidence, the continuing trend toward concentration and centralization. Several giant

At meeting in Paris, Dulles, Eden, and Mendès-France welcome German Chancellor Adenauer, as West Germany becomes 15th member of NATO. West Germany now had full sovereignty and Allied occupation was technically at an end.

U.S. seems to be close to war over Formosan crisis. Chinese Nationalist troops on Quemoy Island, 10 miles off Communist mainland, prepare for possible assault.

Pro-Communist President Jacobo Arbenz of Guatemala loses job after insurrection.
Customs men make him take off his trousers when searching him at frontier.
He was permitted to go to Mexico, later turned up in Europe.

Senator Knowland of California,
outspoken critic of Administration's foreign policy,
wants United States to defend Quemoy and Matsu and vigorously
opposes recognition of Red China.
He leads old Taft wing of Republican party.

New York banks merged. Another trend was the growth of investment in mutual funds. Another (to return to the consumer for a moment) was the flourishing business done by discount houses. Still another factor making for progress was a generally tranquil labor situation.

*　　*　　*

Our most severe worry continued to be foreign policy, that is, relations with our neighbors and how to keep the peace. Sometimes we looked north. At long last—after fifty years, in fact—Congress authorized building of the St. Lawrence Seaway in co-operation with Canada. And events in Latin America concerned us too. Dictator Vargas killed himself in Brazil, and Perón was on the way out in Argentina. An important inter-American conference took place at Caracas, Venezuela, which, under strong US influence, adopted an anti-Communist resolution setting up a kind of new Monroe Doctrine for the Western Hemisphere, to keep

Russian machinations

out. The resolution was adopted seventeen to one, with Mexico and Argentina abstaining and Guatemala negative. Trouble in Guatemala came to a melodramatic head shortly thereafter, and a pro-Communist government was thrown out by a Putsch organized in Honduras, with US help.

President Eisenhower announced during the course of the year that, in the age of the hydrogen bomb, a preventive war was impossible. But we came very close to having to fight in the Far East over Indo-China, when it appeared that Communist China might intervene there and French power continued to weaken. Then, after the fall of Dienbienphu, an event which gave us much emotion, a peace was patched up at Geneva, and the Indo-Chinese Reds were confirmed in their seizure of the northern half of Viet-Nam —60,000 square miles and 14 million people. Later came another "brink of war" crisis over Formosa and the offshore islands. (Adlai Stevenson, when details of this became known, accused Mr. Dulles of playing "Russian roulette" with the life of the nation.) The upshot seemed to be that we promised to defend Formosa in case of Communist attack, but that Chiang Kai-shek

Albert Einstein, profound genius and humanitarian, did not like to be thought of as father of the most terrible engines of destruction ever known. Einstein was theoretician chiefly responsible for sudden transposition of the world from one era to another, but was one of gentlest, noblest of men. Here he consults with his close friend J. Robert Oppenheimer, man who made the first atomic bomb and a physicist almost as renowned and respected by colleagues as Einstein himself. Oppenheimer, accused of being a security risk in sensational "trial," enters AEC building (above) where hearings were held.

was put back on leash again, that is, told that he must not attack the China mainland. Once more, our policy was compromise. But it worked.

The United States signed a defense treaty with Pakistan, which meant giving it arms, and this annoyed Mr. Nehru mightily. The Indian Prime Minister attacked American policy in Asia, said that the United States was as responsible as the Soviet Union for world unrest, charged that the American "collective security" system made trouble and unsettlement everywhere, and asked us to stop testing hydrogen bombs in the Pacific. Not deterred, we announced that we would automatically defend the Philippines if they were attacked, and signed the SEATO (South East Asia) treaty. Meantime there came fierce polemics over seating Communist China in the UN. Senator Knowland advocated withdrawal of the United States from the UN if this happened. The administration disagreed, but did not want to seat Red China either.

As to Europe, the Russians, naturally, wanted to push us out. Molotov offered Europe a 50-year security treaty, with the US excluded; the offer was rejected, and further negotiations seemed like an unending game of catch-as-catch-can. (At about the same time, Russian blandishments were also extended to Japan.) Germany's fate and future remained uncertain. France, after tortuous parliamentary debate, killed the European Defense Community. It looked as if we would have to start all over again, but a new formula was quickly worked out when the British agreed to maintain troops on the European continent without a time limit. Something known as the "Western European Union" was set up, and West Germany, now on its own, joined NATO and was permitted—under certain limitations—to have an army and rearm. Comment from Eisenhower: "One of the greatest diplomatic achievements of our time."

*   *   *

During this year—we are still in **1954**—we were wounded by the perplexities of the Oppenheimer case, a genuine American tragedy. It became known in April that, some months before, Dr. J. Robert Oppenheimer, creator of the atomic bomb, had been suspended as consultant to the Atomic Energy Commission, on the ground that he was a

possible security risk.

Admiral Lewis L. Strauss, chairman of the AEC (who more than once has been criticized for highhandedness), gave Oppenheimer the choice of resignation or facing charges. Oppenheimer chose the latter, and a three-man board conducted an elaborate inquiry. It refused by a two-to-one vote to restore Oppenheimer's security clearance, although it agreed unanimously that he was "loyal." Then the AEC voted four-to-one against reinstating Oppenheimer because of "proof of fundamental defects in his character" and because his previous association with Communists extended beyond the "tolerable limits of prudence and restraint."

The Oppenheimer story has two kernels. One was that he had associated with Communists and ex-Communists. This he freely admitted (his wife was, in fact, a former Communist), but he said he had lost all sympathy with Com-

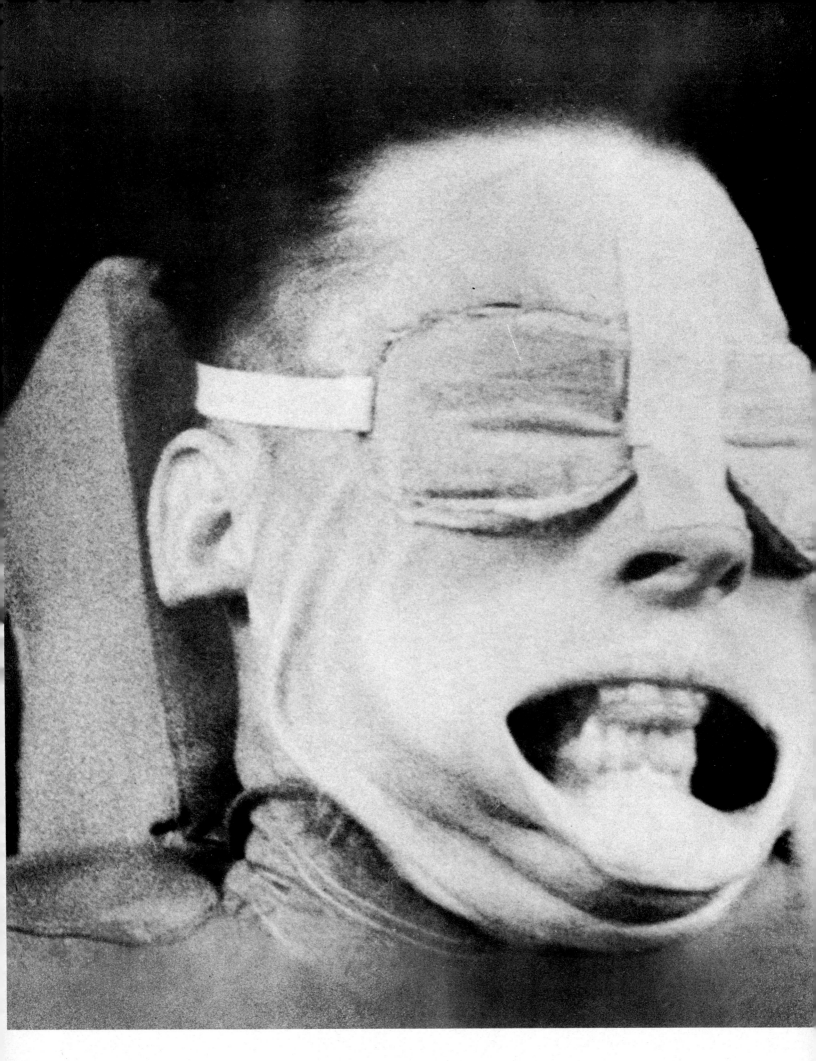

This is what man-made hurricane can do to a human face. Air stream hits navy volunteer undergoing test to see how jet pilots may be better protected when bailing out of planes.

And this is what a non-man-made hurricane can do. Mighty Carol attacked New England and among other things snapped off steeple of Old North Church, Boston, like a match.

munism, and had never in any way participated in subversion. The other was that he had opposed development of the H-bomb when he was chairman of the General Advisory Committee of the AEC, after Mr. Truman's decision to go ahead with it. Oppenheimer denied this. The point raised was of piercing interest. Obviously, it was foolish to say the least for a government servant in Oppenheimer's position to play around with Communists. But was it right that any man should have his character stained and perhaps his life ruined because he disagreed with government policy? If so, we had come to a sorry pass indeed.

The majority report of the Security Board sitting on the case contains the sentence, "The hard requirements of security, and the assertion of freedoms, thrust upon us a dilemma not easily resolved. In the present international situation our security measures exist, in the ultimate analysis, to protect our free institutions." This is well stated, but it begs the question of what may happen if security regulations are abused. Chief Justice Warren wrote once: "Must a nation that is now the strongest in the world demand, for its own further strength and security, a sacrifice by its own citizens of their ancient liberties? This problem haunts the work of all our courts these days. But the Constitution exists for the individual as well as for the nation. I believe it will prove itself adequate to this challenge."

*   *   *

Someone had the pert idea about this time of identifying hurricanes alphabetically by girls' names, and in **1954** we got all the way to T. (What will happen if any year ever has more than 26 hurricanes is unknown.) The most notable this year were Alice, which blasted its way through Texas in June, and Carol, which

was really a monster

for anything bearing such a pretty name. Carol attacked Long Island and New England late in August, swept north along the Atlantic Coast, and made hash of farms and villages. Sixty-eight people were killed; and the damage was a neat $500 million. Then we had the threat of Edna, who blew herself out at sea. But Hazel in October was another savage beauty.

"Pogo" plane rises or descends vertically; Navy will use it as fighter. Like a helicopter, it can land almost anywhere. Speed: 500 miles an hour.

Character in science fiction? No. U.S. fliers in jet age wear something akin to armor.

Thule, Air Force base near North Pole, is "loneliest place in world." Men stationed there longed for something green, get a tree.

These hurricanes were, however, as nothing compared to the winds blowing Eisenhower's popularity to new dimensions. He had come to symbolize and personify our prodigious national success. There were only three issues that mattered—peace, prosperity, and liberty. And, despite some slipshod faltering and sulphurous crises, we had all three.

*　　*　　*

So we reach the doorstep of **1955**, and our ten years are nearly done. Was this great America of ours invincible, as we liked to think? Might we, by the mysterious and unavoidable processes of history, become isolated in time and rendered more vulnerable to martial attack? What good would all our wealth be then? What future were we promising our sons? Obviously, in the case of a surprise H-bomb attack, the American capacity

to retaliate quickly

would depend on the Strategic Air Command and its massive fleet of intercontinental jet bombers. But, it seemed, this fleet was not as big as it should be. General LeMay asked for more giant B-52's to replace the smaller B-47's, and did not get them—at least did not get enough of them to satisfy the S.A.C. A B-52 costs $7 million. The thrust and counterthrust so familiar to American congressional and administrative procedures—need for economy balanced against need for national defense—came into play again, and the Air Force budget was severely trimmed. Meantime we heard that the Soviets were producing many more "Bisons"—their intercontinental bomber—than we were producing B-52's, and were ahead of us in other fields. Not only was their diplomacy clever and farseeing enough to keep us guessing, but they seemed to be doing very well indeed in matching us weapon for weapon. No American had the right to be complacent any more.

General Curtis E. LeMay, hard-boiled head of SAC, has his own flying office, a C-97.

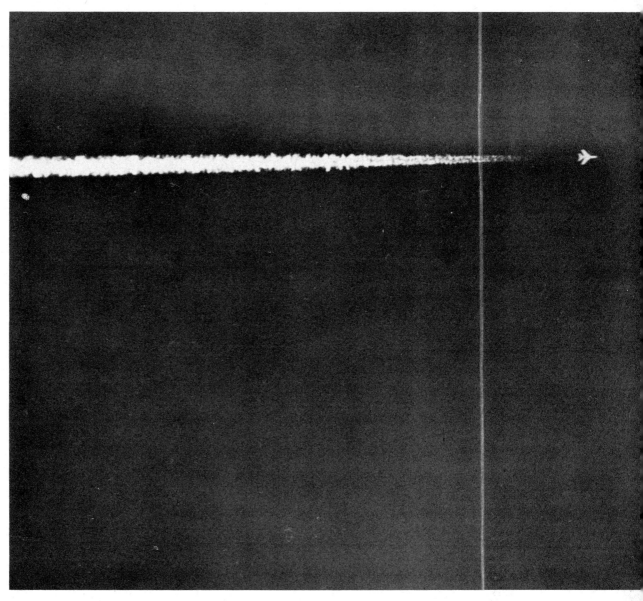

In January, 1955, the world's first atomic submarine, the "Nautilus," underwent first sea trials. She can go around world—30,000 miles—in 50 days on a two-pound lump of uranium the size of a golfball. Ordinary submarines can only stay submerged for about 100 miles at a time. The "Nautilus" is armed with "Regulus," a 7-ton guided missile.

This F-100 C jet, with trail of vapor, is averaging 822.135 miles per hour in level flight, which is a new record for a piloted aircraft and is 160 miles per hour faster than speed of sound. Some American planes go even faster.

Consider the desperately urgent question of guided missiles. Our guided missile program was, critics said, being "starved" at the very time that the Soviets were actually putting into flight tests their 1,500-mile intercontinental ballistic missile. Such weapons with atomic warheads could, in theory, make untenable the American bases in Europe essential to our strategic bombers.

Meantime other atomic developments continued. If war could be averted, it was clear that not only the United States but the entire world was indeed entering a new era, possibly the most

brilliant and productive

in the history of civilization. Seventy-three nations, including both the US and the USSR, met at Geneva under UN auspices for an "atoms-for-peace" conference. Technical secrets were shared with nations not producing atomic energy. At home Congress was urged to appropriate five billion dollars in five years to build atomic power plants for industrial use, since our military stockpile was so big that we had plenty of nuclear fuel to spare.

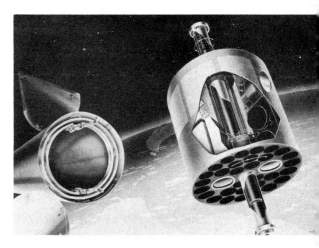

The U.S. is building artificial moons, and one of these satellites will be launched in 1957. If it works, it will whirl around earth at an altitude of about 250 miles once every 90 minutes at speed of 18,000 miles per hour. Could science fiction do better? Yet we took it all in our stride.

Anna Mary ("Grandma") Moses passed her 95th birthday in 1955, and remained an institution as authentic as cracker barrels in village stores. Cracker barrels are going out, but the New England scenes that "Grandma" painted will, if in no other way, survive by virtue of her crisp, friendly art.

In a small Kansas town farmers' wives paint for fun. They have done local scenes often, but one of them says, "The town's still full of pictures."

Vodka martinis become popular. The Cold War continued, but this did not keep people from liking a drink with a good old Russian name.

We amused ourselves with hobbies, like boating (motels for boats came to be known as "marinas"), and amiable

forms of self-expression,

like putting paint on canvas. Americans, as is notorious, take fun very seriously. Kitchen gadgets of new and ingenious variety multiplied, and household articles like plastic wall tiles, coated wire, and laminated pantry surfaces became standard. Safety belts entered automobiles. Cigarettes got longer. Men tended to spend more time fixing the house up. The US, as one observer put it, became the country where the husband did the kitchen work and the wife took over the bank account, while TV narcotized the children.

VistaVision competed with CinemaScope at the movies, and advertisers now spent more than a billion dollars a year on TV shows seen over more than 460 stations. "Oklahoma!" was reborn on the screen with the new Todd-AO process, and "Cinerama Holiday" was the biggest movie moneymaker of the year. Nobody was funnier on TV than Phil Silvers. People in

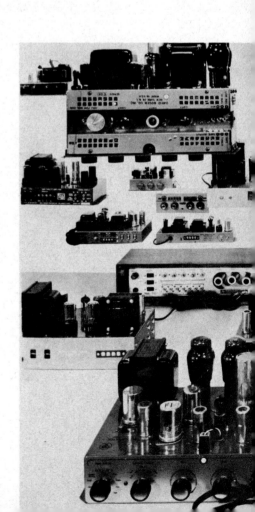

218

"Hi-fi" becomes a lively boom, and so do tape-recorders. Tone-conscious listeners like to assemble their own high-fidelity sets.

On vacations and weekends, automobiles carry boats to the nearest water. More than five million Americans have motorboats.

Johnny Podres, Dodger hero, likes his Corvette. Produced by Chevrolet, it has plastic body, and stands only 33 inches high at the door. The vogue for light, fast sports cars and easily maneuverable European models continued. Counterpart is Ford's Thunderbird.

vast number read "Gift from the Sea," by Anne Morrow Lindbergh. The "Condensed Books" put out by the "Reader's Digest" set dazzling new records for book club distribution. (And the good old "Digest" now took advertising. Some day we might even see the "National Geographic" in a new cover.) Louis Armstrong gave triumphant jazz concerts all over Europe. Youngsters indulged in an animated, sexy dance called Rock 'n Roll. And the Dodgers beat the Yankees to win their first World's Series, probably the most electrifying series ever played.

Sports and entertainment help give the US its infinite, bewildering variety. Maybe we pay too much attention to trivialities and maybe we are victims at times of "push-button civilization," but this is a country not only virile and elastic but independent-minded and, at bottom, profoundly sensible. People make up their own minds in the United States, and phonies do not last long. Our heartbeat is *positive and sound.*

Nashua, potentially biggest moneymaking horse in history, wins $100,000 race against Derby winner Swaps, as owner William Woodward, Jr., and wife Ann watch jubilantly. Woodward was tragically killed later when his wife, thinking he was a prowler in their Long Island home, shot him by accident.

It was hard not to listen to the "$64,000 Question" on Tuesday nights. The first person to win $64,000 was Marine Captain Richard McCutchen, who knew a vast lot about French food and cooking. Another winner was a sensationally erudite amateur expert on boxing, psychologist Dr. Joyce Brothers.

Grace Kelly won an Academy Award, went to the magical Riviera, and met a real-life prince, with the result the world well knows. Not since the Windsors has there been so much romantic commotion, and preparations began for what was called "the wedding of the century."

"Marty" was a "sleeper." It did well on television, for which it was written, but few people knew that it would make history as a movie. One good reason for its success is performance of Ernest Borgnine as the lonely, sentimental butcher.

A new star is born—Susan Strasberg, only 17. Her sureness of touch, sensitiveness, and above all sheer power in "The Diary of Anne Frank" were astonishing. The Broadway season was, incidentally, the most promising and productive in years.

Youngsters everywhere began to go happily and energetically crazy because of Davy Crockett—not the original, but the Walt Disney TV program portraying the adventures of this oldtime frontier hero. Sudden collapse of craze left manufacturers with oversupply of fur caps.

221

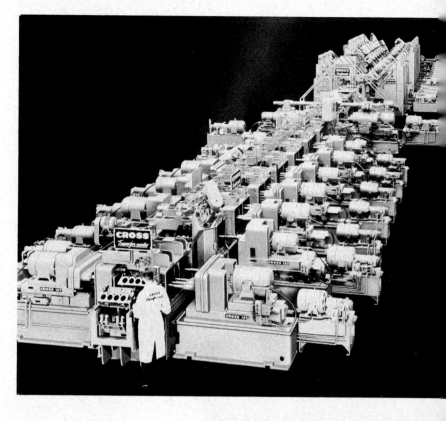

Professor Norbert Wiener, a formidable specialist
in the science of communications, has traced out
recondite analogies between the communication
systems of human bodies and machines.
He invented cybernetics, which led to automation,
and is on the staff of M.I.T.

Enter automation, which may transform
the American industrial scene beyond recognition.
Automation means, in a word, the process whereby
machines, with little help from men, run machines.
One worker can make a machine turn out even the
most complicated machine parts without ever
touching them.

George Meany (above) head of the AF of L, and Walter
Reuther, boss of the CIO (right), merge their organizations
into single huge labor confederation, with 15 million

Mass production of plastic automobiles begins.
Miraculous new plastics were invented, like Mylar,
which is thin as a hair, one-third as strong as
steel, and unbreakable. New foams
(isocyanates) are "soft as a pillow
or as hard as plywood."

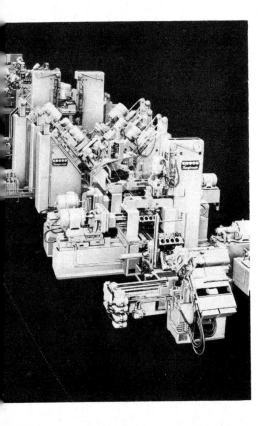

The main news on the domestic front was prosperity. **1955** was called "the biggest boom year in history," and the stock market (not counting one big slip after the announcement of Eisenhower's illness) went right on climbing. It went so high, in fact, that margin requirements were put up to 70 per cent, to discourage speculation, and a Senate committee undertook an investigation of Wall Street to see if it was safe to be as rich as we seemed to be. Stockholders paid little attention, and continued to accumulate dividends. General Motors split its stock three for one, and became the first corporation in history ever to make a net profit of more than a billion dollars in a year. Companies like Standard Oil of New Jersey and US Steel surpassed all their existing records. The gross national output came close to $400 billion, and personal income reached $272 billion, way over 1954.

The wonder of it all

was that so many of us still had trouble paying the grocery bill.

The Ford Foundation announced during the year the largest grant ever made at one time by a philanthropic organization—$500,000,000 allocated to more than 4,000 privately supported universities, colleges, and hospitals.

members. Meany, 61, started life as a plumber; Reuther, 48, won a big victory in 1955 by getting auto companies to accept principle of guaranteed annual wage.

The "hard sell" becomes a familiar phrase.
Executive explains with cheerleader gusto
the virtues of new models coming off the assembly
line, and his sales force listens dutifully.
New cars have to have pep.
So do the salesmen.

223

The late Rabbi Joshua L. Liebman of Boston influenced millions with his "Peace of Mind," first published in 1946, and set a vigorous mode for a new type of self-help book. People read him avidly to get rid of fear, self-doubt, and strain. Liebman combined a religious approach with modern psychology.

Bishop Fulton J. Sheen wrote books like "Three to Get Married," became a radio and TV star, and confirmed his position as one of the most eloquent personalities in the nation. Previously he had won renown by converting many notables to the Catholic faith, like Heywood Broun and Clare Boothe Luce.

Dr. Norman Vincent Peale, Methodist minister, gives homely advice as well as religious inspiration. His book, "The Power of Positive Thinking," broke all records in its field, and his newspaper columns, magazine articles, recorded sermons, and TV appearances added to his huge influence.

At Brandeis University, Waltham, Mass., three chapels have been built—one Protestant, one Catholic, one Jewish—to form a unit.

Distinguished novels have borne such titles as "The Age of Reason" and "The Age of Longing," but a better phrase to epitomize the contemporary era might be "The Age of Anxiety." This has not—to put it mildly—been a carefree decade. A Mayo Clinic doctor said that the stomach ulcer has become "the wound stripe of our civilization," and social security records disclosed that no fewer than eight million US citizens were classified as "neurotic." We lived too fast and in circumstances of too much crowding and pressure. So we sought outlets and palliatives—from reckless driving and sexual uproar to sleeping pills and new drugs like Miltown, which became a craze. It seemed that most of us had to be artificially pepped up on the one hand, and artificially sedated on the other. Some sought

release or consolation

in religion. And religion takes, of course, many forms. The arc is wide between St. Thomas's or St. Patrick's on Fifth Avenue and what might be called the sub-Christian cults of certain primitive Californians. There was no doubt

Each is shaped in the form of a Bible partly open, and the three together symbolize universal faith. Brandeis is Jewish-sponsored but non-sectarian.

Nobody since Billy Sunday has ever drawn such audiences as revivalist Billy Graham, 31. Revivalism has always been authentic part of the American scene, particularly in the southern "Bible-belts." But Graham reached for hearts and souls successfully all over the nation, and in Europe as well.

Bishop Henry Knox Sherrill of the Episcopal Church, a seasoned intellectual, is a far cry from Graham. Another eminent clergyman, sometimes known irreverently as the "Protestants' Sheen," is Dean James A. Pike of the Cathedral of St. John the Divine, New York.

that religious revival and fermentation were going on, if only because so many earnest people sought "peace of mind." Churches were full. Even the most dignified men of God used radio and TV to carry their message further. Books that preached "the cult of reassurance" sold like popcorn in the movies.

The fact remains, according to reliable statistics, that only about half of the people of the United States have even "a nominal relationship to any religious body." America is a country with an unalterable puritan tradition, but our religion is, for the most part, undemonstrative. A recent poll showed that only one-third of American families still say grace at meals. One development perturbing to religious and ethical leaders was an increase in what seemed to be moral apathy or callousness. This was a reflection of the inescapable realities of the Cold War, foreign policy, and the atomic age. The national strategy was based on the concept that, in the event of war, we would be obliged to annihilate at once whole populations—men, women, and children alike—and might be annihilated ourselves. But few people seemed to care, or, if they did care, they didn't show it.

Much continued to happen in the realms of medicine, science, and technology. We could record almost without end such items as that a new chemical element named einsteinium was isolated, that artificial diamonds were manufactured for the first time, and that "atomic particle radiation was used to induce hereditary changes in plants

to make them immune

to certain diseases." Brilliant and diligent researchers were busy on a hundred fronts. But, increasingly, we needed more scientists than we had, many more. It became known that the USSR every year graduated more than twice as many engineers as the US. One suggestion was that, to remedy our critical deficiency, industry should release some of its best scientists to the schools, in order to create "a national scientific reserve." The newspapers were filled with advertisements of a kind never seen before, appeals from aircraft and other companies for rocket and guided missile specialists, aerodynamicists, aerothermodynamicists, digital computer engineers, combustion engineers, and "vibration" and "reliability" engineers.

But the great and happy event of the year in science was application— at last—on a broad national scale of Dr. Salk's vaccine. This was indeed an epochal forward step. The worst of all childhood plagues, infantile paralysis, appeared to be doomed. Parents by the million felt their hearts soar. But this enormous advance did not come without anguishing temporary tribulations. In April the University of Michigan evaluation center, after elaborate mass tests, announced that the vaccine was "safe and effective." At once a national program was set up to inoculate millions of young children. But some early batches of vaccine were defective, and a handful of children died. Later, after inept and extremely unedifying wrangles, inoculation was resumed, and did no appreciable damage. When the stentorian cry for vaccine was at its height Mrs. Oveta Culp Hobby, at that time Secretary of Health, Education and Welfare, pulled a nice little boner by saying that no one had realized how great the immediate demand for it would be.

Dozens of new antibiotics were discovered and put to useful work. Between 1944 and 1954 the death rate from pneumonia was cut by 42 per cent, from tuberculosis 75 per cent. Average life expectancy rose to 69.8 years, double what it was seventy-five years ago. And the birthrate climbed.

And other domestic events got into the crowded pages of newspapers along with pictures of night-club singers with next-to-bare breasts and people cut in half by motor accidents. Congress extended the draft. Mr. Eisenhower asked for lower tariffs on some commodities, a striking thing for a Republican to do, and called for a federal program to build more classrooms for the schools. Senate investigators went after two new targets, the great philanthropic foundations and the newspapers, but found little. A young man, to collect $37,500 insurance on his mother, killed her and 43 others by putting a bomb in an airplane—a novel method of mass murder. Admiral Byrd went to Antarctica again. Air Force Secretary Harold E. Talbott resigned his post. And a number of notable Americans died—including Robert E. Sherwood, Albert Einstein, and Cordell Hull.

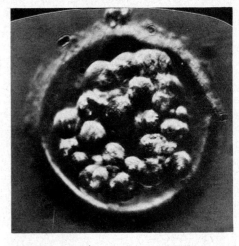

Man presumes to attempt creation of life itself. Picture shows "a three-day-old human embryo artificially cultivated from a fertilized ovum," photographed at the point when scientists had performed miracle of getting it to reach a growth of 32 tiny cells. Then embryo disintegrated.

Dr. Jonas E. Salk inoculates a schoolboy with his polio vaccine. First mass use indicated that the vaccine, a terrific boon, was 80% effective.

An Illinois housewife bursts with excitement when sex-determination test tells her that her unborn child will be a girl. Test, invented in France, depends on analysis of pregnant woman's saliva, takes only a few minutes, and costs $5.00. American physicians remain skeptical.

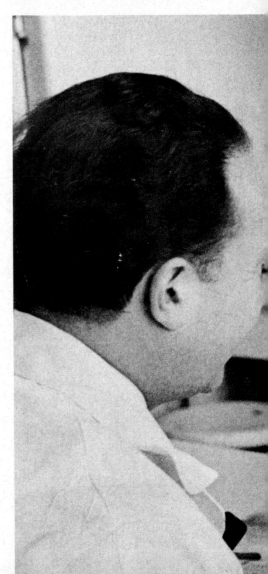

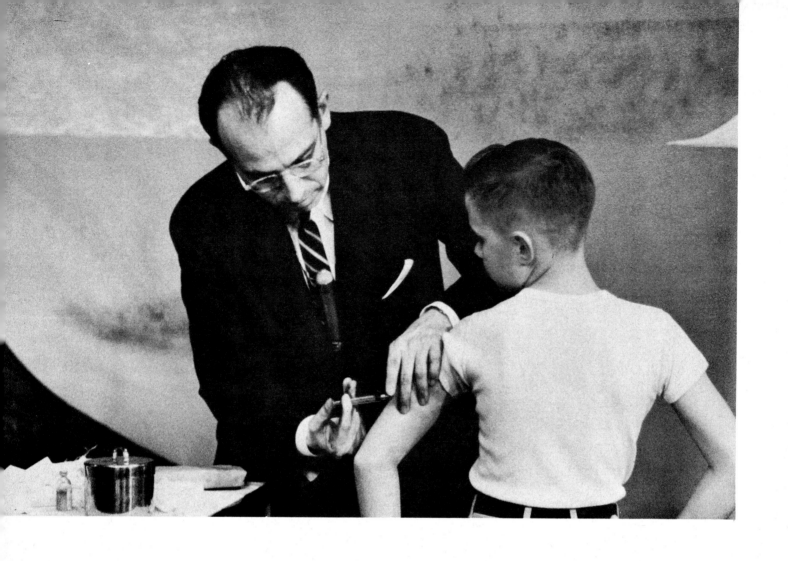

We turn to the record of **1955** in foreign affairs. The Russians seemed to have taken on a "New Look." A Big Four "Summit" Conference took place at Geneva, Switzerland, with Eisenhower, Bulganin, Premier Edgar Faure of France, and Sir Anthony Eden, who had succeeded Churchill as British Prime Minister, participating. This was the first meeting of the great powers on such a level since Potsdam ten years before. The atmosphere was cordial, and everybody agreed that nuclear war was unthinkable. Mr. Eisenhower invited the Russians to join the US in "halting the production of fissionable materials for war," if they would accept an American "open skies" proposal, whereby each country could inspect the other's armament.

Other thorny topics were postponed, but a few chinks in the Iron Curtain were opened, and it seemed for the moment that real peace might be with us at last. The "Geneva spirit" did not, however, flourish very long. "Coexistence" became even more competitive than before.

The Russians set up East Germany, their puppet, as a "free" and "sovereign" state, thus hoping to counterbalance the sovereignty of West Germany. Chancellor Adenauer visited the United States to pay his respects, but he visited Moscow too. And

perplexing troubles

came in other quarters. Almost the whole of the old colonial world seemed to be bursting into nationalist flame, from Algeria to Cyprus and beyond. Americans were lax in not foreseeing this. We had known for some time that, instead of having old friends like England and France in critical contested areas, we might have enemies, or, at best, countries holding fast to a neutralist or "uncommitted" position. But we did not seem to grasp the full realities of this development and the need for taking a new imaginative line. Politics, like nature, abhors a vacuum. If we did not promptly give help to the new nations, with or without political strings, somebody else would. No fewer than 29 African and Asian countries met at Bandung, Indonesia, to explore their situation. Meantime Tunisia and Morocco came close to freedom, and at the other end of the globe Malaya was promised independence soon. Indeed, the world of European mastery was gone forever.

Thirteen American prisoners of Chinese Communists were given sentences ranging from four years to life for "espionage" in November (1954). When news came of their conviction Eisenhower sent telegrams of solicitude to families. Mrs. Harry Benjamin, whose son was a flier shot down near the Yalu, mourns at empty Thanksgiving table.
In August, 1955, boys were released.

Eisenhower and Bulganin meet at "Summit" Conference in Geneva, but results were not altogether encouraging. Personal contact, however, led to subsequent correspondence that may be fruitful and end nuclear stalemate.

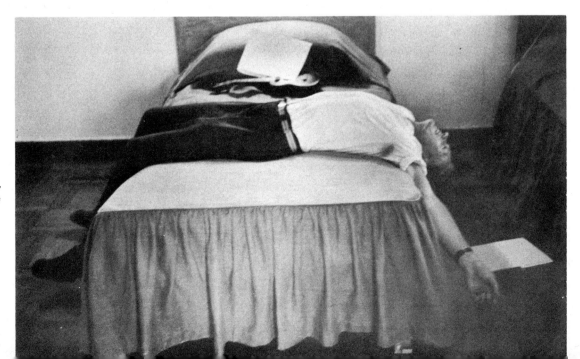

Four other young Americans, held in confinement for more than two years, were also released and deported. Lt. Lyle Cameron collapses happily when he reaches safety in Hong Kong.

Bulganin (left) and Khrushchev visit neutralist India, and get an unparalleled reception. Our own relations with India worsened, following faux pas by Dulles over Goa, a Portuguese enclave in India which Indians claim.

Rug was pulled out from under France in Morocco, and Sultan deposed in 1953 returned triumphantly to the throne. Here Resident General Gronval, attending funeral of a French official in the company of a Moroccan dignitary, indicates acute discomfiture. Nationalist rebels also made grave trouble in Algeria.

Egypt, key to Middle East, also holds to "uncommitted" position. Nile dam (above) may be precursor to projected huge "High Dam" near Aswan, which U.S. agreed to help finance in order to counter-balance Communist sales of arms to Egypt. Meantime deteriorating relations between Egypt and Israel brought war close.

Later in the year, as the result of a complex compromise, sixteen new members entered the UN. Four belonged to the Communist bloc, and six were African or Asian. This was not an American defeat, but we failed, at least for the time being, to gain entrance for Japan.

Egypt in October announced that it would buy arms in large quantities from Communist Czechoslovakia. This was a very severe blow indeed to Western aims and prestige, and it was in part our fault. Active intervention by the Soviets in the Middle East, which they had hitherto ignored, could transform the entire international

balance of power.

What also counted was that the Russians were now using an adroit new tactic in trying to win over the neutralist states, the offer of economic help and capital investment—a field, moreover, in which we had thought ourselves to be supreme. Russia became a competitor not merely in armament, atoms, and diplomacy, but in business. Then Khrushchev and Bulganin visited India, where they paid effective court. Next we heard that the Russians had offered Afghanistan $100 million, which is a lot of money for Afghanistan.

And our security arrangements suffered grave assault. Neutralist Egypt, Syria, and Saudi Arabia, which was richer than rich, set out to undermine the Baghdad Pact, which we supported but hesitated to join. A nasty explosion came in Jordan, which had long been in the British camp. More Soviet aid went to the Arab states, and an Arab war against Israel, which was isolated and without adequate arms, became an ugly possibility. Wash-

Ike kept country on tenterhooks awaiting his decision. A lot of people did not like the idea of a "part-time" President, but, regardless of politics, everybody was happy that the Chief Executive recovered from his illness promptly, was able to take up his responsibilities, and seemed fit and well.

Sec'y of Treasury Humphrey was talked about as a possible candidate if President decided not to run.

Harold Stassen, Eisenhower's adviser on disarmament, might have been in the running too.

Chief Justice Warren would have been ideal candidate, if Ike stepped out, but wanted to stay on the Court.

Gov. Christian A. Herter of Mass. was talked of as a Vice-Presidential candidate if Nixon withdrew.

Senator Knowland and Vice-President Nixon talk over the situation. Another California politico much in the picture was Governor Goodwin J. Knight.

ington did not want to promote an arms race in the Middle East, but we did a lot of dillydallying which did not help us on either side.

On September 24, 1955, the nation was stunned to hear that President Eisenhower, vacationing in Denver, had suffered a heart attack. The country was as shocked as if it, so to speak, had had a heart attack, and messages expressing concern and grief poured in from every corner of the world. The President was moved from his mother-in-law's home to Fitzsimmons Army Hospital, and went into an oxygen tent. He made an excellent recovery, under the supervision of a corps of physicians headed by Dr. Paul Dudley White of Boston, and on November 7 was well enough to fly back to Washington. The President said, "I am happy that the doctors have given me a parole, if not a pardon, and I expect to be back at my accustomed duties, although they say I must ease and not bulldoze my way into them." There followed six more weeks of convalescence in Gettysburg, and then several brief vacations in the South.

No one wanted to take political advantage of the illness of a beloved President, but the issue had to be faced—was Mr. Eisenhower going to be well enough to run, if he wanted to run, for a second term in 1956? This question obliterated all other questions. Candidates for the succession gathered. There is good reason to believe, now, that the President had been inclined not to run again before his illness, strange as this may seem. And Republican hearts sank at some of his declarations while he was still convalescing. He said frankly, "It would be idle to pretend that my health can be wholly restored," and, "My life must be carefully regulated to avoid excessive fatigue."

Opponents of the President felt strongly that no man who was not totally up to the job of being President should risk damaging his health—to say nothing of the country—by running. The real question was not, as one distinguished columnist put it, one of death or disability but of "inadequacy."

Mr. Eisenhower, an utterly conscientious man, wrestled soberly for week after week with his *agonizing decision.*

Shortly after the turn of the year he told the American nation on TV that he would run if the people wanted him, and promised to step out if he became seriously ill again.

Democratic candidates found this an agonizing period too. If Eisenhower did not run, any Democrat had a good chance of winning. With Ike in the race, the situation was quite different. Adlai Stevenson, who continued to distinguish himself for temperateness but who suffered from his unwillingness to offer people the moon, announced his candidacy, and Estes Kefauver pressed him close. Dark horses arose, and the race appeared to be wide open.

Stevenson and Kefauver were the outstanding Democratic candidates. Governor Harriman did not campaign actively, but would not say "No."

Two prominent Democratic governors, with powerful political backing, were Lausche of Ohio (left) and Meyner of New Jersey (right). Also country watched dark horses like Clement of Tennessee, Williams of Mich., Mayor Wagner of N.Y. and particularly Lyndon Johnson (Texas) and Stuart Symington (Mo.).

Some 32 million American children go to public school, far more than present facilities can handle. More than 60,000 new classrooms were built last year, but the country needed 52,000 more. In one California town, as pictured above, a row of tents had to do for classrooms. At least half a million children only went to school half a day, and schools operated in double or even triple shifts. But in spite of all this the standards of American public school education were probably the highest in the world.

The American farm crisis is perennial, and Secretary of Agriculture Benson had the most thankless job in the Cabinet. Big farms ate up little farms in the Middle West, and Congress wrangled over parity. Democratic aspirants for the Presidency hammered on the administration's farm policy. But, even if prices fell and farmers complained, the earth was rich. We produced too much, not too little. The inexhaustible vitality of the American earth, its indestructible fruitfulness, are factors never to be ignored.

We had other problems too. An astounding number of Americans still live in physical circumstances little short of disgraceful. Slums, far from having been conquered, eat their way further into great cities. Above is glimpse of a condemned area in a Chicago neighborhood, only a few blocks away from shining skyscrapers.

And the Negro problem remained the worst of all. Innumerable communities refused to give civic rights, social justice, and a fair break to Negroes. Here the mother of Emmett Till weeps by his coffin. Till was a 14-year-old boy murdered in Mississippi because "he whistled at a white woman." His assassins were acquitted.

Perhaps the United States is too big, too various, too new, too animated, to generalize about. But as a matter of fact, although indubitably big, we are not by any means the biggest nation in the world, and, by contemporary standards, we are not particularly new. One distinguishing mark, impossible to contradict, is American vitality—the sheer overwhelming appetite for life, for the full radiant enjoyment of living, that most Americans have, and want to pass on undiminished to their children. Another is the confusion in real values,

the perplexity in aim,

that vitality and variety are apt to bring. America is one nation, but is also many nations—a rainbow land.

Certainly we have problems. This book is a record of how we have dealt with some of them. The most embracing of them all, it hardly needs be said, is how to master and utilize our own inherent power, our own giant and abundant forces, to make a free, productive, happy life for all.

To sum up this crowded, stunning decade in the life of the greatest country on earth in a few bony words is not easy. As well try to push a football into a matchbox. But a brace of tentative statements may be made. How well did we meet the challenges that faced us ten years ago, when we were all, so it seems now, 30 or 40 years younger?

First, our economy expanded beyond measure, and we positively reeked of wealth. Employment reached 65 million, more than the New Deal promised in its rosiest dreams. (True, we still had what appears to be a permanent unabsorbable core of about 2.2 million **un**employed.) The budget was not balanced, and the national debt was rising, but few citizens seemed to care. Moreover the prodigious gains in the national economy came with no serious infringement on the social benefits won by the broad mass of the people in the previous decade. In fact, social benefits continued to advance.

Floods whipped through the Atlantic states once again, roaring rivers swept over their banks, whole towns were wrecked. Damage: a billion dollars.

Second, in spite of everything, we remained a free country run by free men under free institutions—a democracy. Civil liberties underwent as serious an attack as any in our history, but survived. And the Communist conspiracy was unmasked and beaten down.

Third, we stopped predatory Communism dead in its tracks in Korea, but we lost heavily elsewhere in the Cold War. On balance—but the equilibrium changed from month to month, even from day to day—it seemed that we were holding even with the Russians, but only just. Unless men in Washington and Main Street woke up, used more imagination, and appreciated more

Disasters both natural and unnatural may recur, but life goes on. An entranced father

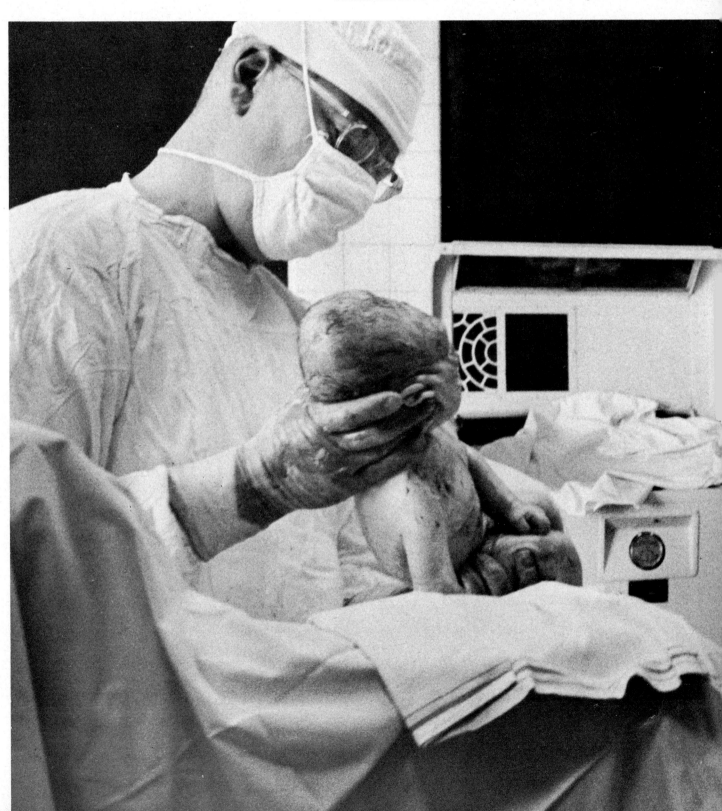

the aspirations of peoples everywhere, we might well lose the rest of the uncommitted world. Of course it was our duty to be strong. It was also our duty to work for peace with discrimination, zest, and intelligence.

Fourth, despite discomfitures, we enjoyed ourselves. It is too much to ask a nation of *160,000,000 people* to be a single happy family, but we tried. Our pregnant hopes, our dreams, remained illimitable. Anyway we had lived through it all. And it was certainly one heck of a decade.

Husband and wife clutch at their small child, as foaming waters advanced. In some areas flood reached a crest as high as a three-story building.

watches his son being born. The baby is one second old, and the mother looks content.

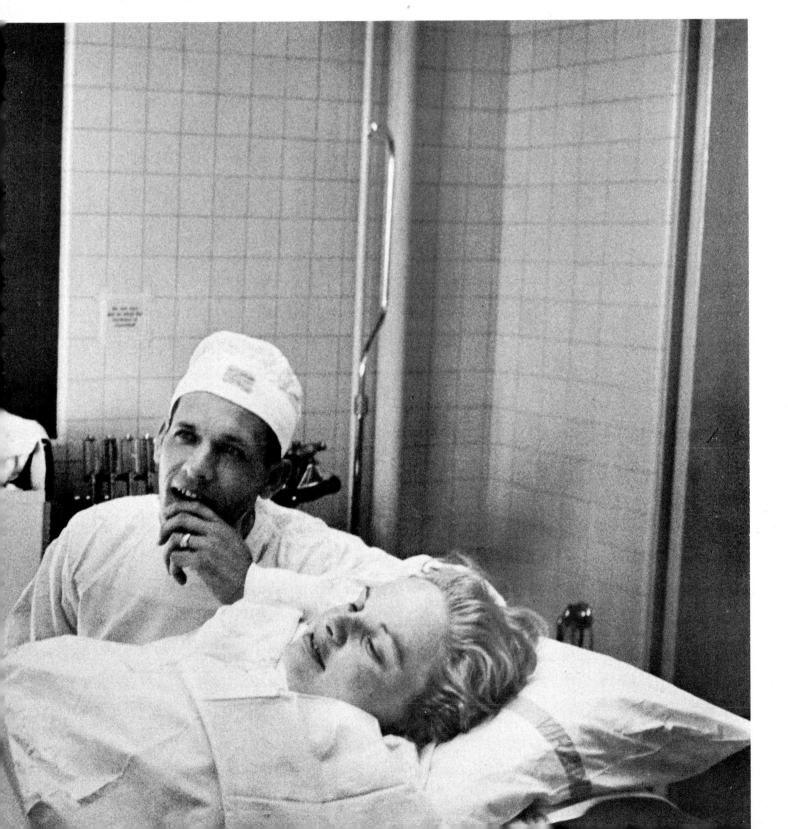

Picture
Credits

The following list by pages shows the source from which each picture was obtained. Where several sources appear on one page, pictures from left to right are separated by commas; from top to bottom, by dashes; unless otherwise indicated. Wherever pictures are not credited, sources prefer anonymity.

Abbreviations: cen., center; lt., left; rt., right; B.S., Black Star; G.H., Graphic House; Int., International; U.P., United Press; W.W., Wide World.

6 W.W.
7 **Miami Herald**—W.W.—Int.
8-9 Mediterranean Allied Air Force, **Life:** William Vandivert
10 **Life:** Ralph Morse
11 U.P., U.S. Army Signal Corps—**Life:** William Shrout
12 **Life:** Alfred Eisenstaedt—**Life:** Sam Shere
13 U.P.
14 Joint Task Force One—M.I.T. Radiation Lab.
15 **Life:** George Skadding
16 **Life:** James Laughead, **Life:** Frank Scherschel
17 **Life:** Margaret Bourke-White, **Life:** David Scherman
18 **Life:** Edward Clark
19 Los Angeles **Times** photo by Art Rogers, **Life:** Peter Stackpole—U.P.—W.W., **Life:** Albert Fenn
20-21 Int., **Life:** Jack Wilkes—**Life:** Dmitri Kessel, W.W.
22-23 **Life:** Nina Leen, **Life:** Myron H. Davis, **Life:** Nina Leen—W.W., **Life:** Harold Carter, **Life:** Frank Scherschel
24-25 U.P., **Life:** Edward Clark—W.W., U.P.
26-27 lt. W.W.; cen. **Life:** Yale Joel; W.W.—**Life:** George Lacks— **Life:** Hank Walker
28-29 **Life:** Hank Walker, N.Y. **Daily News** from Gilloon Agency
30 **Life:** Bob Landry
31 Paramount Pictures (2)—Samuel Goldwyn
32 **Life:** Edward Clark—N.Y. **Daily News** from Gilloon Agency—**Life:** Edward Clark
33 Int.
34 **Life:** Nina Leen
35 **Life:** Sharland—**Life:** James Laughead
36-37 **Life:** James Birns from G.H., W.W.—**Life:** Alfred Eisenstaedt, **Life:** Leonard McCombe
38 **Life:** Eric Schaal
39 U.P.—**Life:** Yale Joel
40-41 lt. **Life:** James Laughead—**Life:** Martha Holmes; cen. **Life:** Martha Holmes; U.P.— **Life:** Martha Holmes—**Life:** Frank Scherschel
42 **Life:** George Silk—W.W.—U.P.
43 **Life:** Larry Burrows
44-45 **Life:** Andreas Feininger, **Life:** Arnold Newman ©—W.W.
46-47 **Life:** James Burke
48 **Life:** Dmitri Kessel—W.W. (2)
49 Fenno Jacobs from B.S.
50-51 Ford Motor Company Archives, **Life:** Jack Birns from G.H., **Life:** Anthony Linck—**Life:** Loomis Dean
52-53 lt. **Life:** Eric Schaal, cen. **Life:** Albert Fenn, Skippy Adelman from B.S.—Neefus from B.S.
54 Courtesy of RCA Laboratories
55 **Life:** Ralph Morse—**Life:** Bernard Hoffman—**Life:** Fritz Goro
56 **Life:** James Eyerman, **Life:** Jerry Cooke from **Pix**—**Life:** Wallace Kirkland—courtesy Cypress Gardens, 20th Century-Fox
57 **Life:** Eric Schaal
58-59 U.P., Harris & Ewing—**Life:** Thomas McAvoy, **Life:** Martha Holmes
60 **Life:** Eliot Elisofon
61 **Life:** Gjon Mili, **Life:** Philippe Halsman—Gaston Longet for RKO Radio Pictures
62-63 Warner Brothers, "Kon-Tiki" Expedition—Rand McNally
64-65 W.W., **Life:** Joe Scherschel—Don Holston, **Life:** Eric Schaal
66 Caroline Valenta
67 Tim Timmerman from the Indianapolis **Times**

68 U.P.—**Life:** Werner Wolff from B.S.
69 W.W.—N.Y. **Daily Mirror** photo from Int.
70-71 U.P., **Life:** W. Eugene Smith—W.W.
72-73 U.P. (3)—Steve Lasker
74 Rue Faris Drew
75 lt. courtesy Knoll Associates, Richard Neutra, Architect—Julius Shulman—**Life:** Loomis Dean
76-77 **Life:** Frank Scherschel, **Life:** Loomis Dean —U.P., **Life:** Andreas Feininger
78 **Life:** Roger Coster from Rapho-Guillumette,
79 **Life:** W. Eugene Smith, **Life:** Edmund B. Gerard—W.W.
80 Int., **Life:** Myron H. Davis—**Life:** Gordon Parks, **Life:** Lisa Larsen
81 **Life:** Martha Holmes
82-83 **Life:** Frank Scherschel, **Life:** Myron H. Davis, W.W.
84-85 M. Rudolph Vetter, **Life:** John Dominis— **Life:** Edward Clark
86-87 **Life:** Cornell Capa, U.P.—W.W., **Life:** Howard Sochurek, W.W., U.P.
88 **Life:** Edmund B. Gerard
89 W.W., Roy Stevens—**Life:** Thomas McAvoy— **Life:** Jack Birns
90-91 lt. Mayer-Burstyn Inc. for De Sica Productions—**Life:** Eileen Darby from G.H.; cen. **Life:** W. Eugene Smith (2),—**Life:** Edward Clark
92-93 **Life:** Nina Leen, **Life:** Ralph Morse
94-95 Werner Wolff from B.S.—CBS, European— **Life:** Ralph Morse, **Life:** Barney Cowherd
96-97 Mathew Zimmerman from W.W.—Int., W.W.
98 **Life:** Carl Mydans
99 **Life:** Thomas McAvoy—W.W.
100-101 **Life:** Dmitri Kessel, Meldolesi from B.S.— J.J. Angleton, John M. Schuller
102-103 Harris & Ewing, Wellington for Kansas City **Star**—**Life:** J. R. Eyerman, Harris & Ewing
104 Int., no credit, **Life:** Hank Walker—**Life:** Michael Rougier—**Life:** R.W. Kelley
105 **Life:** R.W. Kelley
106 **Life:** Carl Mydans
107 W.W. (2)
108 **Life:** Ralph Crane
109 **Life:** David Douglas Duncan, **Life:** Ralph Morse—**Life:** Carl Mydans—**Life:** George Skadding
110-111 **Life:** Hank Walker, **Life:** David Douglas Duncan—**Life:** George Skadding, U.S.A.F. Photo
112 **Life:** David Douglas Duncan
113 **Life:** George Silk, Eastfoto, **Life:** John Dominis
114-115 lt. U.P.; cen. **Life:** Hank Walker; **Life:** Joe Scherschel (2)
116 **Life:** Peter Stackpole, W.W. (3)
117 **Life:** Gjon Mili
118-119 W.W., **Life:** Mark Kauffman—N.Y. **Daily Mirror** photo from Int.
120-121 Myron H. Davis for Columbia Pictures— European, **Life:** Edward Clark, Lippman for Columbia Pictures, U.P.
122-123 W.W., **Life:** Michael Rougier—U.P., **Life:** Hank Walker
124 Illustration by A. Leydenfrost
125 Dept. of Justice—Keystone—W.W.
126-127 Int. (3)
128-129 **Life:** Jack Birns, W.W.
130-131 W.W.—Alexander G. Henderson from Du Pont, **Life:** Carl Iwasaki
132 Arthur Sasse from Int.
133 W.W., **Life:** Margaret Bourke-White
134 Bob Landry—**Life:** Mark Kauffman
135 **Life:** Ralph Morse
136 U.P.
137 W.W., **Life:** Leonard McCombe—W.W. (2)
138-139 W.W., Underwood & Underwood, **Life:** Dmitri Kessel
140 Carl Hart, Jr.—**Life:** Gordon Parks— Mt. Wilson-Palomar
141 **Life:** J.R. Eyerman
142-143 United Artists, **Life:** Philippe Halsman— **Life:** W. Eugene Smith, Andrey Andersson from B.S.
144 **Life:** Gordon Parks
145 W.W.—Int.—**Life:** Peter Stackpole
146-147 U.P., W.W.—Max Peter Haas from European, U.P.
148-149 **Life:** Hy Peskin (2)—W.W., **Life:** Ralph Morse
150-151 lt. **Life:** Hy Peskin; cen. **Life:** Joe Clark; **Life:** Nina Leen—**Life:** Werner Wolff from B.S.
152 Jean Salze of Studio Pereire
153 Underwood & Underwood
154-155 W.W.—**Life:** John Swope

156 W.W.—**Life:** George Skadding—**Life:** Hank Walker
157 **Life:** George Skadding—U.P.
158-159 lt. Free Lance Photographers Guild, rt. British Information Services—U.P.
160 U.P.
161 W.W.
162-163 lt. W.W. (2), rt. Bill Sanders from Miami **Herald**
164-165 lt. **Life:** Yale Joel—Gilloon Agency, rt. Int. (2)—**Life:** John Zimmerman
166-167 Courtesy Desi Arnaz, Slim Aarons, **Life:** Joe Scherschel—Slim Aarons
168 **Life:** Mark Shaw
169 U.P. (2)
170-171 U.P., **Life:** Gordon Tenney
172 European
173 **Life:** Leonard McCombe
174-175 W.W., **Life:** Fritz Goro—no credit, **Life:** Fritz Goro
176-177 Gilloon Agency, Sovfoto—The **New York Times,** W.W.
178-179 **Life:** Howard Sochurek, no credit—P.N. Sharma
180 **Life:** Jun Miki
181 W.W., no credit—**Life:** Michael Rougier— U.P.
182-183 lt. W.W. (2); rt. Hack Miller for Seattle **Post Intelligencer**
184-185 **Life:** N. R. Farbman, Vernon Pick—Mainichi Shimbun, Vernon Pick
186 Atomic Energy Commission
187 courtesy General Electric
188 **Life:** J. R. Eyerman
189 Standard Oil Co. (N.J.)—California Highways and Public Works
190 W.W.—Int.—W.W., **Life:** Nina Leen
191 Graham Moulton, **Life:** Charles Steinheimer
192-193 Sy Friedman for NBC (2)—**Life:** Walter Sanders
194-195 Larry Barbier from Globe Photos, Sam Shaw for 20th Century-Fox, **Life:** Leonard McCombe, **Life:** Alfred Eisenstaedt
196 **Life:** Gordon Parks
197 **Life:** Hank Walker (2)—W.W.
198 **Life:** Lisa Larsen—W.W.
199 **Life:** Hank Walker
200-201 **Life:** Yale Joel, **Life:** Lloyd Turner—W.W., Gilloon Agency
202 **Life:** George Skadding
203 W.W., U.P.
204-205 lt. **Life:** Ralph Morse; cen. W.W. (2)
206-207 lt. European; cen. **Life:** Walter Sanders, rt. **Life:** George Skadding, **Life:** Alfred Eisenstaedt
208 U.P.—Gey—Arthur Shay for **Time**
209 **Life:** Howard Sochurek
210 **Life:** Alfred Eisenstaedt
211 **Life:** Robert Phillips
212 U.S. Navy
213 Joe Spalino from W.W.
214 Lockheed Aircraft Corporation, U.P.— **Life:** George Silk
215 **Life:** A. Y. Owen
216 **Life:** Ralph Morse
217 Courtesy North American Aviation— Illustration by R. Klepp
218-219 Bert Stern, courtesy Ste. Pierre Smirnoff Fls. Inc., CBS-TV, **Life:** Grey Villet— **Life:** Arnold Newman ©, **Life:** R. W. Kelley
220 **Life:** Grey Villet—**Life:** Myron H. Davis
221 **Life:** Sharland, **Life:** Yale Joel—United Artists Productions, **Life:** Leonard McCombe, **Life:** Ralph Morse
222-223 **Life:** Alfred Eisenstaedt, The Cross Company —**Life:** Gordon Coster, **Life:** Leonard McCombe, **Life:** R.W. Kelley
224-225 lt. **Life:** Albert Fenn— **Life:** Mark Kauffman (2); cen. **Life:** Lawrence Lowry; rt. **Life:** John Dominis—**Life:** Walter Sanders
226-227 Dr. Landrum Shettles Columbia-Presbyterian Medical Center N.Y., **Life:** Albert Fenn— **Life:** Wallace Kirkland
228 **Life:** Hank Walker
229 **Life:** A. Y. Owen—**Life:** Howard Sochurek
230 **Life:** James Burke—**Life:** Eliot Elisofon
231 **Life:** James Sadovy
232 **Life:** Carl Iwasaki—**Life:** Mark Kauffman, **Life:** Michael Rougier, **Life:** Verner Reed (2)
233 **Life:** Edward Clark, U.P., **Life:** John Dominis
234-235 lt. **Life:** Allan Grant—**Life:** Edward Clark; cen. **Life:** Fritz Goro; rt. W.W.
236-237 Thomas Dexter Stevens from Providence **Journal Bulletin,** W.W.—**Life:** Burton Glinn

Index by Subjects